FEDERAL RULES OF PROCEDURE WITH FIFTH CIRCUIT INTERNAL OPERATING PROCEDURES

Federal Rules of Appellate Procedure (Effective December 1, 2011), Fifth Circuit Rules and Internal Operating Procedures (IOP) (As amended through October 2011)

Table of Rules

TITLE I. APPLICABILITY OF RULES

	FRAP	5TH CIR. R.	I.O.P.
SCOPE OF RULES; TITLE	1		
Scope of Rules	1(a)		
[Abrogated]	1(b)		
Title	1(c)		
SUSPENSION OF RULES	2		

TITLE II. APPEAL FROM A JUDGMENT OR ORDER OF A DISTRICT COURT

	FRAP	5TH CIR. R.	I.O.P.
APPEAL AS OF RIGHT — HOW TAKEN	3		3
Filing the Notice of Appeal	3(a)		
Joint or Consolidated Appeals	3(b)		
Contents of the Notice of Appeal	3(c)		
Serving the Notice of Appeal	3(d)		
Payment of Fees	3(e)		
APPEAL FROM A JUDGMENT OF A MAGISTRATE JUDGE IN A CIVIL CASE [Abrogated]	3.1		
APPEAL AS OF RIGHT — WHEN TAKEN	4		
Appeal in a Civil Case	4(a)		
Appeal in a Criminal Case	4(b)		
Appeal by an Inmate Confined in an Institution	4(c)		
Mistaken Filing in the Court of Appeals	4(d)		

	FRAP	**5TH CIR. R.**	**I.O.P.**
APPEAL BY PERMISSION	5	5	
Petition for Permission to Appeal	5(a)		
Contents of the Petition; Answer or Cross-Petition; Oral Argument	5(b)		
Form of Papers; Number of Copies	5(c)		
Grant of Permission; Fees; Cost Bond; Filing the Record	5(d)		
APPEAL BY LEAVE UNDER 28 U.S.C. § 636(c)(5) [Abrogated]	5.1		
APPEAL IN A BANKRUPTCY CASE FROM A FINAL JUDGMENT, ORDER, OR DECREE OF A DISTRICT COURT OR BANKRUPTCY APPELLATE PANEL	6		
Appeal From a Judgment, Order, or Decree of a District Court Exercising Original Jurisdiction in a Bankruptcy Case	6(a)		
Appeal From a Judgment, Order, or Decree of a District Court or Bankruptcy Appellate Panel Exercising Appellate Jurisdiction in a Bankruptcy Case	6(b)		
BOND FOR COSTS ON APPEAL IN A CIVIL CASE	7		
STAY OR INJUNCTION PENDING APPEAL	8		
Motion for Stay	8(a)		
Proceeding Against a Surety	8(b)		
Stay in a Criminal Case	8(c)		
Procedures in Death Penalty Cases Involving Applications for Immediate Stay of Execution and Appeals in Matters in Which the District Court Has Either Entered or Refused To Enter a Stay		8	
Documents Required		8.1	
Panels		8.2	

	FRAP	**5TH CIR. R.**	**I.O.P.**
Motions to Vacate Stays		8.3	
Emergency Motions		8.4	
Merits		8.5	
Consideration of Merits		8.6	
Vacating Stays		8.7	
Mandate		8.8	
Stays of Execution Following Decision		8.9	
Time Requirements for Challenges to Death Sentences and/or Execution Procedures		8.10	
RELEASE IN A CRIMINAL CASE	9	9	
Release Before Judgment of Conviction	9(a)	9.1	
Release After Judgment of Conviction	9(b)	9.2	
Criteria for Release	9(c)		
Required Documents		9.3	
Service		9.4	
Response		9.5	
THE RECORD ON APPEAL	10	10	
Composition of the Record on Appeal	10(a)		
The Transcript of Proceedings	10(b)		
Statement of the Evidence When the Proceedings Were Not Recovered or When a Transcript Is Unavailable	10(c)		
Agreed Statement as the Record on Appeal	10(d)		
Correction or Modification of the Record	10(e)		
Appellant's Duty to Order the Transcript		10.1	
Form of Record		10.2	
Transcript Purchase Order			foll. 10.2
FORWARDING THE RECORD	11	11	
Appellant's Duty	11(a)		
Duties of Reporter and District Clerk	11(b)		
Retaining the Record Temporarily in the District Court for Use in Preparing the Appeal	11(c)		
[Abrogated]	11(d)		
Retaining the Record by Court Order	11(e)		
Retaining Parts of the Record in the District Court by Stipulation of the Parties	11(f)		
Record for a Preliminary Motion in the Court of Appeals	11(g)		
Duties of Court Reporters		11.1	

	FRAP	**5TH CIR. R.**	**I.O.P.**
Requests for Extensions of Time		11.2	
Duty of the Clerk		11.3	
Transcript Monitoring			foll. 11.3
DOCKETING THE APPEAL; FILING A REPRESENTATION STATEMENT; FILING THE RECORD	12	12	
Docketing the Appeal	12(a)		
Filing a Representation Statement	12(b)		
Filing the Record, Partial Record, or Certificate	12(c)		

TITLE III. REVIEW OF A DECISION OF THE UNITED STATES TAX COURT

REVIEW OF A DECISION OF THE TAX COURT	13		
How Obtained; Time for Filing Notice of Appeal	13(a)		
Notice of Appeal; How Filed	13(b)		
Contents of the Notice of Appeal; Service; Effect of Filing and Service	13(c)		
The Record on Appeal; Forwarding; Filing	13(d)		
APPLICABILITY OF OTHER RULES TO THE REVIEW OF A TAX COURT DECISION	14		

TITLE IV. REVIEW OR ENFORCEMENT OF AN ORDER OF AN ADMINISTRATIVE AGENCY, BOARD, COMMISSION, OR OFFICER

REVIEW OR ENFORCEMENT OF AN AGENCY ORDER HOW OBTAINED; INTERVENTION	15	15	
Petition for Review; Joint Petition	15(a)		
Application or Cross-Application to Enforce an Order; Answer; Default	15(b)		
Service of the Petition or Application	15(c)		

	FRAP	**5TH CIR. R.**	**I.O.P.**
Intervention	15(d)		
Payment of Fees	15(e)		
Docketing Fee and Copy of Orders			
Agency Review Proceedings		15.1	
Proceedings for Enforcement of Orders of			
the National Labor Relations Board		15.2	
Proceedings for Review of Orders of the Federal			
Energy Regulatory Commission (FERC)		15.3	
Proceedings for Review of Orders of the			
Benefits Review Board		15.4	
Time for Filing Motion for Intervention		15.5	
BRIEFS AND ORAL ARGUMENT IN A NATIONAL LABOR RELATIONS BOARD PROCEEDING	15.1		
THE RECORD ON REVIEW OR ENFORCEMENT	16		
Composition of the Record	16(a)		
Omissions From or Misstatements in the Record	16(b)		
FILING THE RECORD	17	17	
Agency to File; Time for Filing; Notice of Filing	17(a)		
Filing What Constitutes	17(b)		
STAY PENDING REVIEW	18		
Motion for a Stay	18(a)		
Bond	18(b)		
SETTLEMENT OF A JUDGMENT ENFORCING AN AGENCY ORDER IN PART	19		
APPLICABILITY OF RULES TO THE REVIEW OR ENFORCEMENT OF AN AGENCY ORDER	20		

TITLE V. EXTRAORDINARY WRITS

	FRAP	**5TH CIR. R.**	**I.O.P.**
WRITS OF MANDAMUS AND PROHIBITION AND OTHER EXTRAORDINARY WRITS	21	21	

	FRAP	5TH CIR. R.	I.O.P.

Mandamus or Prohibition to a Court:
    Petition, Filing, Service, and Docketing   21(a)
Denial; Order Directing Answer;
    Briefs; Precedence   21(b)
Other Extraordinary Writs   21(c)
Form of Papers; Number of Copies   21(d)

TITLE VI. HABEAS CORPUS; PROCEEDINGS IN FORMA PAUPERIS

HABEAS CORPUS AND SECTION
    2255 PROCEEDINGS   22   22
Application for the Original Writ   22(a)
Certificate of Appealability   22(b)
Cross Reference to 5TH CIR. R. 27.3
    Concerning Emergency Motions   foll. 22(b)
CUSTODY OR RELEASE OF A
    PRISONER IN A HABEAS
    CORPUS PROCEEDING   23
Transfer of Custody Pending Review   23(a)
Detention or Release Pending Review of
    Decision Not to Release   23(b)
Release Pending Review of Decision
    Ordering Release   23(c)
Modification of the Initial Order on Custody   23(d)
Cross Reference to 5TH CIR. R. 9.2 for
    Bail Applications   foll. 23(d)
PROCEEDINGS IN FORMA PAUPERIS   24
Leave to Proceed in Forma Pauperis   24(a)
Leave to Proceed In Forma Pauperis on
    Appeal or Review of an Administrative-
    Agency Proceeding   24(b)
Leave to Use Original Record   24(c)

TITLE VII. GENERAL PROVISIONS

FILING AND SERVICE   25   25
Filing   25(a)

	FRAP	**5TH CIR. R.**	**I.O.P.**
Service of All Papers Required	25(b)		
Manner of Service	25(c)		
Proof of Service	25(d)		
Number of Copies	25(e)		
Facsimile Filing		25.1	
Electronic Filing		25.2	
Electronic Noticing		25.3	
Cross Reference to 5TH CIR. R. 39.2 for Allowable Mailing Costs			foll. 25.3
COMPUTING AND EXTENDING TIME	26	26	
Computing Time	26(a)		
Extending Time	26(b)		
Additional Time after Service	26(c)		
Computing Time		26.1	
Extensions of Time		26.2	
CORPORATE DISCLOSURE STATEMENT	26.1	26.1.1	
Who Must File	26.1(a)		
Time for Filing; Supplemental Filing	26.1(b)		
Number of Copies	26.1(c)		
MOTIONS	27	27	
In General	27(a)		
Disposition of a Motion for a Procedural Order	27(b)		
Power of a Single Judge to Entertain a Motion	27(c)		
Form of Papers; Page Limits; and Number of Copies	27(d)		
Oral Argument	27(e)		
Clerk May Rule on Certain Motions		27.1	
Single Judge May Rule on Certain Motions		27.2	
Emergency Motions		27.3	
Form of Motions		27.4	
Motions to Expedite Appeal		27.5	
Typeface and Type Styles for Motions			foll. 27.5
General Standards for Ruling on Motions			foll. 27.5
Motions Panels			foll. 27.5
Distribution			foll. 27.5

	FRAP	5TH CIR. R.	I.O.P.
To Judges			foll. 27.5
Emergency Motions			foll. 27.5
Motions After Assignment to Calendar			foll. 27.5
Post-Decision Motions			foll. 27.5
Extension of Time To File Petition for Rehearing or Leave To File Out of Time			foll. 27.5
Stay or Recall of Mandate			foll. 27.5
Motion To Amend, Correct, or Settle the Judgment			foll. 27.5
Remand from Supreme Court of the United States			foll. 27.5
BRIEFS	28	28	
Appellant's Brief	28(a)		
Appellee's Brief	28(b)		
Reply Brief	28(c)		
References to Parties	28(d)		
References to the Record	28(e)		
Reproduction of Statutes, Rules, Regulations, etc.	28(f)		
Reserved	28(g)		
Reserved	28(h)		
Briefs in a Case Involving Multiple Appellants or Appellees	28(i)		
Citation of Supplemental Authorities	28(j)		
Briefs Technical Requirements		28.1	
Briefs Contents		28.2	
Brief Order of Contents		28.3	
Supplemental Briefs		28.4	
Signing the Brief		28.5	
Pro Se Briefs		28.6	
Citation to Unpublished Opinions, Orders, etc		28.7	
Miscellaneous Brief Information			foll. 28.6
Acknowledgment of Briefs			foll. 28.6
Sample Briefs and Record Excerpts			foll. 28.6
Checklist Available			foll. 28.6
Cross-Appeals	28.1		
Applicability	28.1(a)		
Designation of Appellant	28.1(b)		
Briefs	28.1(c)		

	FRAP	**5TH CIR. R.**	**I.O.P.**
Cover	28.1(d)		
Length	28.1(e)		
Time to Serve and File a Brief	28.1(f)		
BRIEF OF AN AMICUS CURIAE	29	29	
When Permitted	29(a)		
Motion for Leave to File	29(b)		
Contents and Form	29(c)		
Length	29(d)		
Time for Filing	29(e)		
Reply Brief	29(f)		
Oral Argument	29(g)		
Time for Filing Motion		29.1	
Contents and Form		29.2	
Length of Briefs		29.3	
Denial of Amicus Curiae Status		29.4	
Cross Reference to 5TH CIR. R. 31.2 for Time for Filing			foll. 29.4
APPENDIX TO THE BRIEFS	30	30	
Appellant's Responsibility	30(a)		
All Parties' Responsibilities	30(b)		
Deferred Appendix	30(c)		
Format of the Appendix	30(d)		
Reproduction of Exhibits	30(e)		
Appeal on the Original Record Without an Appendix	30(f)		
Records on Appeal/Record Excerpts/ Appendix Appeals from District Courts, the Tax Court, and Agencies		30.1	
Appendix Agency Review Proceedings		30.2	
SERVING AND FILING BRIEFS	31	31	
Time to Serve and File a Brief	31(a)		
Number of Copies	31(b)		
Consequence of Failure to File	31(c)		
Briefs Number of Copies; Computer Generated Briefs		31.1	
Briefs Time for Filing Briefs of Intervenors or Amicus Curiae		31.2	
Briefs Time for Mailing or Delivery to a Commercial Carrier		31.3	
Briefs Time for Filing		31.4	

	FRAP	**5TH CIR. R.**	**I.O.P.**
Limits on Extensions of Time to File Briefs			foll. 31.4.4
FORM OF BRIEFS, APPENDICES, AND OTHER PAPERS	32	32	
Form of a Brief	32(a)		
Form of an Appendix	32(b)		
Form of Other Papers	32(c)		
Signature	32(d)		
Local Variation	32(e)		
Typeface		32.1	
Type Volume Limitations		32.2	
Certificate of Compliance		32.3	
Motions for Extra-Length Briefs		32.4	
Rejection of Briefs and Record Excerpts		32.5	
Cross Reference to 5TH CIR. R. 30 Form of Record Excerpts/Appendix			foll. 32.5
CITING JUDICIAL DISPOSITIONS	32.1		
APPEAL CONFERENCES	33		
Cross Reference to 5TH CIR. R. 15.3.5 Regarding Prehearing Conferences			foll. 33
ORAL ARGUMENT	34	34	
In General	34(a)		
Notice of Argument; Postponement	34(b)		
Order and Contents of Argument	34(c)		
Cross-Appeals and Separate Appeals	34(d)		
Nonappearance of a Party	34(e)		
Submission on Briefs	34(f)		
Use of Physical Exhibits at Argument; Removal	34(g)		
Docket Control		34.1	
Oral Arguments		34.2	
Submission Without Argument		34.3	
Number of Counsel To Be Heard		34.4	
Expediting Appeals		34.5	
Continuance of Hearing		34.6	
Recording of Oral Arguments		34.7	
Criminal Justice Act Cases		34.8	
Checking In with Clerk s Office		34.9	
Submission Without Argument		34.10	
Time for Oral Argument		34.11	
Additional Time for Oral Argument		34.12	

	FRAP	**5TH CIR. R.**	**I.O.P.**
Calling the Calendar		34.13	
Screening			foll. 34.13
Decision Without Oral Argument			foll. 34.13
Court Year Schedule			foll. 34.13
Judge Assignments			foll. 34.13
Panel Selection Procedure			foll. 34.13
Separation of Assignment of Judges and Calendaring of Cases			foll. 34.13
Preparation and Publishing Calendars			foll. 34.13
General			foll. 34.13
Calendaring by Case Type			foll. 34.13
Preference Cases			foll. 34.13
Non-preference Cases			foll. 34.13
Calendaring for Convenience of Counsel			foll. 34.13
Number of Cases Assigned			foll. 34.13
Advance Notice			foll. 34.13
Forwarding Briefs to Judges			foll. 34.13
Pre-Argument Preparation			foll. 34.13
Identity of Panel			foll. 34.13
Oral Argument			foll. 34.13
Presenting Argument			foll. 34.13
Lighting Signal Procedure			foll. 34.13
Appellant's Argument			foll. 34.13
Appellee's Argument			foll. 34.13
Appellant's Rebuttal			foll. 34.13
Case Conferences and Designation of Writing Judge			foll. 34.13
EN BANC DETERMINATION	35	35	
When Hearing or Rehearing En Banc May Be Ordered	35(a)		
Petition for Hearing or Rehearing En Banc	35(b)		
Time for Petition for Hearing or Rehearing En Banc	35(c)		
Number of Copies	35(d)		

	FRAP	**5TH CIR. R.**	**I.O.P.**
Response	35(e)		
Call for a Vote	35(f)		
Caution		35.1	
Form of Petition		35.2	
Response to Petition		35.3	
Time and Form Extensions		35.4	
Length		35.5	
Determination of Causes En Banc and Composition of En Banc Court		35.6	
Petition for Rehearing En Banc			foll. 35.6
Extraordinary Nature of Petitions for Rehearing En Banc			foll. 35.6
The Most Abused Prerogative			foll. 35.6
Handling of Petition by the Judges			foll. 35.6
Panel Has Control			foll. 35.6
Requesting a Poll			foll. 35.6
Requesting a Poll on Court's Own Motion			foll. 35.6
Polling the Court			foll. 35.6
Negative Poll			foll. 35.6
Affirmative Poll			foll. 35.6
No Poll Request			foll. 35.6
Capital Cases			foll. 35.6
ENTRY OF JUDGMENT; NOTICE	36		
Entry	36(a)		
Notice	36(b)		
INTEREST ON JUDGMENT	37		
When the Court Affirms	37(a)		
When the Court Reverses	37(b)		
FRIVOLOUS APPEAL DAMAGES AND COSTS	38		
COSTS	39	39	
Against Whom Assessed	39(a)		
Costs For and Against the United States	39(b)		
Costs of Copies	39(c)		
Bill of Costs: Objections; Insertion in Mandate	39(d)		
Costs on Appeal Taxable in the District Court	39(e)		

	FRAP	**5TH CIR. R.**	**I.O.P.**
Taxable Rates		39.1	
Nonrecovery of Mailing and Commercial Delivery Service Costs		39.2	
Time for Filing Bills of Costs		39.3	
PETITION FOR PANEL REHEARING	40	40	
Time to File; Contents; Answer; Action by the Court if Granted	40(a)		
Form of Petition; Length	40(b)		
Copies		40.1	
Limited Nature of Petition for Panel Rehearing		40.2	
Length		40.3	
Time for Filing		40.4	
Necessity for Filing			foll. 40.4
Capital Cases			foll. 40.4
MANDATE: CONTENTS; ISSUANCE AND EFFECTIVE DATE; STAY	41	41	
Contents	41(a)		
When Issued	41(b)		
Effective Date	41(c)		
Staying the Mandate	41(d)		
Stay of Mandate — Criminal Appeals		41.1	
Recall of Mandate		41.2	
Effect of Granting Rehearing En Banc		41.3	
Issuance of Mandate in Expedited Appeals or Mandamus Actions		41.4	
When Mandate Issues, Generally and Specific Instances			foll. 41.4
VOLUNTARY DISMISSAL	42	42	
Dismissal in the District Court	42(a)		
Dismissal in the Court of Appeals	42(b)		
Dismissal by Appellant		42.1	
Frivolous and Unmeritorious Appeals		42.2	
Dismissal for Failure to Prosecute		42.3	
Dismissals Without Prejudice		42.4	
SUBSTITUTION OF PARTIES	43		
Death of a Party	43(a)		
Substitution for a Reason Other Than Death	43(b)		

	FRAP	**5TH CIR. R.**	**I.O.P.**
Public Officer: Identification; Substitution	43(c)		
CASES INVOLVING A CONSTITUTIONAL QUESTION WHEN THE UNITED STATES OR THE RELEVANT STATE IS NOT A PARTY	44		
Constitutional Challenge to Federal Statute	44(a)		
Constitutional Challenge to State Statute	44(b)		
CLERK'S DUTIES	45	45	
General Provisions	45(a)		
Records	45(b)		
Notice of an Order or Judgment	45(c)		
Custody of Records and Papers	45(d)		
Location		45.1	
Release of Original Papers		45.2	
Office To Be Open		45.3	
Office Hours and Phone Numbers			foll. 45.3
ATTORNEYS	46	46	
Admission to the Bar	46(a)		
Suspension or Disbarment	46(b)		
Discipline	46(c)		
Admission and Fees		46.1	
Suspension or Disbarment		46.2	
Entry of Appearance		46.3	
Disciplinary Action			foll. 46.3
Duties of Court Appointed Counsel			foll. 46.3
LOCAL RULES BY COURTS OF APPEALS	47		
Local Rules	47(a)		
Procedure When There Is No Controlling Law	47(b)		
OTHER FIFTH CIRCUIT RULES		47	
Name, Seal and Process		47.1	
Sessions		47.2	
Circuit Executive, Library and Staff Attorneys		47.3	
Bankruptcy Appeals		47.4	
Publication of Opinions		47.5	
Affirmance Without Opinion		47.6	

	FRAP	**5TH CIR. R.**	**I.O.P.**
Calendaring Priorities		47.7	
Attorney's Fees		47.8	
Rules for the Conduct of Proceedings Under the Judicial Conduct and Disability Act, 28 U.S.C. §§ 351 et seq.		47.9	
Rule Governing Appeals Raising Sentencing Guidelines Issues 18 U.S.C. § 3742		47.10	
MASTERS	48		
Appointment; Powers	48(a)		
Compensation	48(b)		
OTHER INTERNAL OPERATING PROCEDURES			foll. 48
Judicial Council			foll. 48
Judicial Conference			foll. 48
Lawyers Advisory Committee			foll. 48
Recusal or Disqualification of Judges			foll. 48
Special Panels and Cases Requiring Special Handling			foll. 48
Corporate Reorganization Chapter 11			foll. 48
Criminal Justice Act Plan			foll. 48
Certified Records for Supreme Court of the United States			foll. 48
Building Security			foll. 48

APPENDIX OF FORMS

Form

1. Notice of Appeal to a Court of Appeals From a Judgment or Order of a District Court.
2. Notice of Appeal to a Court of Appeals From a Decision of the United States Tax Court.
3. Petition for Review of Order of an Agency, Board, Commission or Officer.
4. Affidavit Accompanying Motion for Permission to Appeal In Forma Pauperis.
5. Notice of Appeal to a Court of Appeals From a Judgment or Order of a District Court or a Bankruptcy Appellate Panel.
6. Certificate of Compliance with Rule 32(a).

FED. R. APP. P. WITH 5TH CIR. R. & IOPs

FEDERAL RULES OF APPELLATE PROCEDURE, 5TH CIR. R. and INTERNAL OPERATING PROCEDURES
(Effective December 1, 2011)

TITLE I. APPLICABILITY OF RULES

FRAP 1. SCOPE OF RULES; TITLE

(a) *Scope of Rules.*

    (1) These rules govern procedure in the United States courts of appeals.

    (2) When these rules provide for filing a motion or other document in the district court, the procedure must comply with the practice of the district court.

(b) **Definition.** In these rules, state includes the District of Columbia and any United States commonwealth or territory.

(c) *Title.* These rules are to be known as the Federal Rules of Appellate Procedure.

FRAP 2. SUSPENSION OF RULES

On its own or a party's motion, a court of appeals may — to expedite its decision or for other good cause — suspend any provision of these rules in a particular case and order proceedings as it directs, except as otherwise provided in Rule 26(b).

TITLE II. APPEAL FROM A JUDGMENT OR ORDER OF A DISTRICT COURT

FRAP 3. APPEAL AS OF RIGHT — HOW TAKEN

(a) *Filing the Notice of Appeal.*

(1) An appeal permitted by law as of right from a district court to a court of appeals may be taken only by filing a notice of appeal with the district clerk within the time allowed by Rule 4. At the time of filing, the appellant must furnish the clerk with enough copies of the notice to enable the clerk to comply with Rule 3(d).

(2) An appellant s failure to take any step other than the timely filing of a notice of appeal does not affect the validity of the appeal, but is ground only for the court of appeals to act as it considers appropriate, including dismissing the appeal.

(3) An appeal from a judgment by a magistrate judge in a civil case is taken in the same way as an appeal from any other district court judgment.

(4) An appeal by permission under 28 U.S.C. § 1292(b) or an appeal in a bankruptcy case may be taken only in the manner prescribed by Rules 5 and 6, respectively.

(b) *Joint or Consolidated Appeals.*

(1) When two or more parties are entitled to appeal from a district-court judgment or order, and their interests make joinder practicable, they may file a joint notice of appeal. They may then proceed on appeal as a single appellant.

(2) When the parties have filed separate timely notices of appeal, the appeals may be joined or consolidated by the court of appeals.

(c) *Contents of the Notice of Appeal.*

(1) The notice of appeal must:

(A) specify the party or parties taking the appeal by naming each one in the caption or body of the notice, but an attorney representing more than one party may describe those parties with such terms as "all plaintiffs," "the defendants," "the plaintiffs A, B, et al.," or "all defendants except X";

(B) designate the judgment, order, or part thereof being appealed; and

(C) name the court to which the appeal is taken.

(2) A pro se notice of appeal is considered filed on behalf of the signer and the signer s spouse and minor children (if they are parties), unless the notice clearly indicates otherwise.

(3) In a class action, whether or not the class has been certified, the notice of appeal is sufficient if it names one person qualified to bring the appeal as representative of the class.

(4) An appeal must not be dismissed for informality of form or title of the notice of appeal, or for failure to name a party whose intent to appeal is otherwise clear from the notice.

(5) Form 1 in the Appendix of Forms is a suggested form of a notice of appeal.

(d) *Serving the Notice of Appeal.*

(1) The district clerk must serve notice of the filing of a notice of appeal by mailing a copy to each party's counsel of record   excluding the appellant's   or, if a party is proceeding pro se, to the party s last known address. When a defendant in a criminal case appeals, the clerk must also serve a copy of the notice of appeal on the defendant, either by personal service or by mail addressed to the defendant. The clerk must promptly send a copy of the notice of appeal and of the docket entries   and any later docket entries   to the clerk of the court of appeals named in the notice. The district clerk must note, on each copy, the date when the notice of appeal was filed.

(2) If an inmate confined in an institution files a notice of appeal in the manner provided by Rule 4(c), the district clerk must also note the date when the clerk docketed the notice.

(3) The district clerk's failure to serve notice does not affect the validity of the appeal. The clerk must note on the docket the names of the parties to whom the clerk mails copies, with the date of mailing. Service is sufficient despite the death of a party or the party's counsel.

(e) *Payment of Fees.* Upon filing a notice of appeal, the appellant must pay the district clerk all required fees. The district clerk receives the appellate docket fee on behalf of the court of appeals.

FIFTH CIRCUIT RULE 3

Filing Fee. When the notice of appeal is filed, the $455 fees established by 28 U.S.C. §§ 1913 and 1917 must be paid to the district court clerk. After the Fifth Circuit receives a duplicate copy of a notice of appeal, the clerk will send counsel or a party notice advising of other requirements of the rule. No additional fees are required. Failure to pay the fees does not prevent the appeal from being docketed, but is grounds for dismissal under 5TH CIR. R. 42.

FRAP 3.1. APPEAL FROM A JUDGMENT OF A MAGISTRATE JUDGE IN A CIVIL CASE

[Abrogated]

FRAP 4. APPEAL AS OF RIGHT — WHEN TAKEN

(a) *Appeal in a Civil Case.*

    (1) *Time for Filing a Notice of Appeal.*

        (A) In a civil case, except as provided in Rules 4(a)(1)(B), 4(a)(4), and 4(c), the notice of appeal required by Rule 3 must be filed with the district clerk within 30 days after entry of the judgment or order appealed from.

        (B) The notice of appeal may be filed by any party within 60 days after entry of the judgment or order appealed from if one of the parties is:

            (i) the United States;

            (ii) a United States agency;

            (iii) a United States officer or employee sued in an official capacity; or

            (iv) a current or former United States officer or employee sued in an individual capacity for an act or omission occurring in connection with duties performed on the United States behalf including all instances in which the United States represents that person when the judgment or order is entered or files the appeal for that person.

        (C) An appeal from an order granting or denying an application for a writ of error *coram nobis* is an appeal in a civil case for purposes of Rule 4(a).

    (2) *Filing Before Entry of Judgment.* A notice of appeal filed after the court announces a decision or order but before the entry of the judgment or order is treated as filed on the date of and after the entry.

    (3) *Multiple Appeals.* If one party timely files a notice of appeal, any other party may file a notice of appeal within 14 days after the date when the first notice was filed, or within the time otherwise prescribed by this Rule 4(a), whichever period ends later.

    (4) *Effect of a Motion on a Notice of Appeal.*

        (A) If a party timely files in the district court any of the following motions under the Federal Rules of Civil Procedure, the time to file an appeal runs for all parties from the entry of the order disposing of the last such remaining motion:

(i) for judgment under Rule 50(b);

(ii) to amend or make additional factual findings under Rule 52(b), whether or not granting the motion would alter the judgment;

(iii) for attorney s fees under Rule 54 if the district court extends the time to appeal under Rule 58;

(iv) to alter or amend the judgment under Rule 59;

(v) for a new trial under Rule 59; or

(vi) for relief under Rule 60 if the motion is filed no later than 28 days after the judgment is entered.

(B) (i) If a party files a notice of appeal after the court announces or enters a judgment but before it disposes of any motion listed in Rule 4(a)(4)(A) the notice becomes effective to appeal a judgment or order, in whole or in part, when the order disposing of the last such remaining motion is entered.

(ii) A party intending to challenge an order disposing of any motion listed in Rule 4(a)(4)(A), or a judgment's alteration or amendment upon such a motion, must file a notice of appeal, or an amended notice of appeal in compliance with Rule 3(c) within the time prescribed by this Rule measured from the entry of the order disposing of the last such remaining motion.

(iii) No additional fee is required to file an amended notice.

(5) *Motion for Extension of Time.*

(A) The district court may extend the time to file a notice of appeal if:

(i) a party so moves no later than 30 days after the time prescribed by this Rule 4(a) expires; and

(ii) regardless of whether its motion is filed before or during the 30 days after the time prescribed by this Rule 4(a) expires, that party shows excusable neglect or good cause.

(B) A motion filed before the expiration of the time prescribed in Rule 4(a)(1) or (3) may be ex parte unless the court requires otherwise. If the motion is filed after the expiration of the prescribed time, notice must be given to the other parties in accordance with local rules.

(C) No extension under this Rule 4(a)(5) may exceed 30 days after the prescribed time or 14 days after the date when the order granting the motion is entered, whichever is later.

(6) *Reopening the Time to File an Appeal.* The district court may reopen the time to file an appeal for a period of 14 days after the date when its order to reopen is entered, but only if all the following conditions are satisfied:

(A) the court finds that the moving party did not receive notice under Federal Rule of Civil Procedure 77(d) of the entry of the judgment or order sought to be appealed within 21 days after entry;

(B) the motion is filed within 180 days after the judgment or order is entered or within 14 days after the moving party receives notice under Federal Rule of Civil Procedure 77(d) of the entry, whichever is earlier; and

(C) the court finds that no party would be prejudiced.

(7) *Entry Defined.*

(A) A judgment or order is entered for purposes of this Rule 4(a):

(i) if Federal Rule of Civil Procedure 58(a) does not require a separate document, when the judgment or order is entered in the civil docket under Federal Rule of Civil Procedure 79(a); or

(ii) if Federal Rule of Civil Procedure 58(a) requires a separate document, when the judgment or order is entered in the civil docket under Federal Rule of Civil Procedure 79(a) and when the earlier of these events occurs:

- the judgment or order is set forth on a separate document, or

- 150 days have run from entry of the judgment or order in the civil docket under Federal Rule of Civil Procedure 79(a).

(B) A failure to set forth a judgment or order on a separate document when required by Federal Rule of Civil Procedure 58(a) does not affect the validity of an appeal from that judgment or order.

(b) *Appeal in a Criminal Case.*

(1) *Time for Filing a Notice of Appeal.*

(A) In a criminal case, a defendant's notice of appeal must be filed in the district court within 14 days after the later of:

(i) the entry of either the judgment or the order being appealed; or

(ii) the filing of the government s notice of appeal.

(B) When the government is entitled to appeal, its notice of appeal must be filed in the district court within 30 days after the later of:

(i) the entry of the judgment or order being appealed; or

(ii) the filing of a notice of appeal by any defendant.

(2) *Filing Before Entry of Judgment.* A notice of appeal filed after the court announces a decision, sentence, or order but before the entry of the judgment or order is treated as filed on the date of and after the entry.

(3) *Effect of a Motion on a Notice of Appeal.*

(A) If a defendant timely makes any of the following motions under the Federal Rules of Criminal Procedure, the notice of appeal from a judgment of conviction must be filed within 14 days after the entry of the order disposing of the last such remaining motion, or within 14 days after the entry of the judgment of conviction, whichever period ends later. This provision applies to a timely motion:

(i) for judgment of acquittal under Rule 29;

(ii) for a new trial under Rule 33, but if based on newly discovered evidence, only if the motion is made no later than 14 days after the entry of the judgment; or

(iii) for arrest of judgment under Rule 34.

(B) A notice of appeal filed after the court announces a decision, sentence, or order but before it disposes of any of the motions referred to in Rule 4(b)(3)(A) becomes effective upon the later of the following:
(i) the entry of the order disposing of the last such remaining motion; or

(ii) the entry of the judgment of conviction.

(C) A valid notice of appeal is effective without amendment to appeal from an order disposing of any of the motions referred to in Rule 4(b)(3)(A).

(4) *Motion for Extension of Time.* Upon a finding of excusable neglect or good cause, the district court may before or after the time has expired, with or without motion and notice extend the time to file a notice of appeal for a period not to exceed 30 days from the expiration of the time otherwise prescribed by this Rule 4(b).

(5) *Jurisdiction.* The filing of a notice of appeal under this Rule 4(b) does not divest a district court of jurisdiction to correct a sentence under Federal Rule of Criminal Procedure 35(a), nor does the filing of a motion under 35(a) affect the validity of a notice of appeal filed before entry of the order disposing of the motion. The filing of a motion under Federal Rule of Criminal Procedure 35(a) does not suspend the time for filing a notice of appeal from a judgment of conviction.

(6) *Entry Defined.* A judgment or order is entered for purposes of this Rule 4(b) when it is entered on the criminal docket.

(c) *Appeal by an Inmate Confined in an Institution.*

(1) If an inmate confined in an institution files a notice of appeal in either a civil or a criminal case, the notice is timely if it is deposited in the institution s internal mail system on or before the last day for filing. If an institution has a system designed for legal mail, the inmate must use that system to receive the benefit of this rule. Timely filing may be shown by a declaration in compliance with 28 U.S.C. § 1746 or by a notarized statement, either of which must set forth the date of deposit and state that first-class postage has been prepaid.

(2) If an inmate files the first notice of appeal in a civil case under this Rule 4(c), the 14-day period provided in Rule 4(a)(3) for another party to file a notice of appeal runs from the date when the district court dockets the first notice.

(3) When a defendant in a criminal case files a notice of appeal under this Rule 4(c), the 30-day period for the government to file its notice of appeal runs from the entry of the judgment or order appealed from or from the district court's docketing of the defendant's notice of appeal, whichever is later.

(d) *Mistaken Filing in the Court of Appeals.* If a notice of appeal in either a civil or a criminal case is mistakenly filed in the court of appeals, the clerk of that court must note on the notice the date when it was received and send it to the district clerk. The notice is then considered filed in the district court on the date so noted.

FRAP 5. APPEAL BY PERMISSION

(a) *Petition for Permission to Appeal.*

(1) To request permission to appeal when an appeal is within the court of appeals discretion, a party must file a petition for permission to appeal. The petition must be filed with the circuit clerk with proof of service on all other parties to the district-court action.

(2) The petition must be filed within the time specified by the statute or rule authorizing the appeal or, if no such time is specified, within the time provided by Rule 4(a) for filing a notice of appeal.

(3) If a party cannot petition for appeal unless the district court first enters an order granting permission to do so or stating that the necessary conditions are met, the district court may amend its order, either on its own or in response to a party s motion, to include the required permission or statement. In that event, the time to petition runs from entry of the amended order.

(b) *Contents of the Petition; Answer or Cross-Petition; Oral Argument.*

(1) The petition must include the following:

(A) the facts necessary to understand the question presented;

(B) the question itself;

(C) the relief sought;

(D) the reasons why the appeal should be allowed and is authorized by a statute or rule; and

(E) an attached copy of:

(i) the order, decree, or judgment complained of and any related opinion or memorandum, and

(ii) any order stating the district court s permission to appeal or finding that the necessary conditions are met.

(2) A party may file an answer in opposition or a cross-petition within 10 days after the petition is served.

(3) The petition and answer will be submitted without oral argument unless the court of appeals orders otherwise.

(c) *Form of Papers; Number of Copies.* All papers must conform to Rule 32(c)(2). Except by the court's permission, a paper must not exceed 20 pages, exclusive of the disclosure statement, the proof of service, and the accompanying documents required by Rule 5(b)(1)(E). An original and 3 copies must be filed unless the court requires a different number by local rule or by order in a particular case.

(d) *Grant of Permission; Fees; Cost Bond; Filing the Record.*

(1) Within 14 days after the entry of the order granting permission to appeal, the appellant must:

(A) pay the district clerk all required fees; and

(B) file a cost bond if required under Rule 7.

(2) A notice of appeal need not be filed. The date when the order granting permission to appeal is entered serves as the date of the notice of appeal for calculating time under these rules.

(3) The district clerk must notify the circuit clerk once the petitioner has paid the fees. Upon receiving this notice, the circuit clerk must enter the appeal on the docket. The record must be forwarded and filed in accordance with Rules 11 and 12(c).

FIFTH CIRCUIT RULE 5

Length. *The certificate of interested persons required by 5TH CIR. R. 28.2.1 does not count toward the page limit.*

FRAP 5.1. APPEAL BY LEAVE UNDER 28 U.S.C. § 636(c)(5)

[Abrogated]

FRAP 6. APPEAL IN A BANKRUPTCY CASE FROM A FINAL JUDGMENT, ORDER, OR DECREE OF A DISTRICT COURT OR BANKRUPTCY APPELLATE PANEL

(a) *Appeal From a Judgment, Order, or Decree of a District Court Exercising Original Jurisdiction in a Bankruptcy Case.* An appeal to a court of appeals from a final judgment, order, or decree of a district court exercising jurisdiction under 28 U.S.C. § 1334 is taken as any other civil appeal under these rules.

(b) *Appeal From a Judgment, Order, or Decree of a District Court or Bankruptcy Appellate Panel Exercising Appellate Jurisdiction in a Bankruptcy Case.*

  (1) *Applicability of Other Rules.* These rules apply to an appeal to a court of appeals under 28 U.S.C. § 158(d) from a final judgment, order, or decree of a district court or bankruptcy appellate panel exercising appellate jurisdiction under 28 U.S.C. § 158(a) or (b). But there are 3 exceptions:

  (A) Rules 4(a)(4), 4(b), 9, 10, 11, 12(b), 13-20, 22-23, and 24(b) do not apply;

  (B) the reference in Rule 3(c) to "Form 1 in the Appendix of Forms" must be read as a reference to Form 5; and

  (C) when the appeal is from a bankruptcy appellate panel, the term "district court," as used in any applicable rule, means appellate panel.

  (2) *Additional Rules.* In addition to the rules made applicable by Rule 6(b)(1), the following rules apply:

  (A) *Motion for rehearing.*

   (i) If a timely motion for rehearing under Bankruptcy Rule 8015 is filed, the time to appeal for all parties runs from the entry of the order disposing of the motion. A notice of appeal filed after the district court or bankruptcy appellate panel announces or enters a judgment, order, or decree but before disposition of the motion for rehearing becomes effective when the order disposing of the motion for rehearing is entered.

   (ii) Appellate review of the order disposing of the motion requires the party, in compliance with Rules 3(c) and 6(b)(1)(B), to amend a previously filed notice of appeal. A party intending to challenge an altered or amended judgment, order, or decree must file a notice of appeal or amended notice of appeal within the time prescribed by Rule 4 excluding Rules 4(a)(4) and 4(b) measured from the entry of the order disposing of the motion.

(iii) No additional fee is required to file an amended notice.

(B) *The record on appeal.*

(i) Within 14 days after filing the notice of appeal, the appellant must file with the clerk possessing the record assembled in accordance with Bankruptcy Rule 8006 and serve on the appellee a statement of the issues to be presented on appeal and a designation of the record to be certified and sent to the circuit clerk.

(ii) An appellee who believes that other parts of the record are necessary must, within 14 days after being served with the appellant's designation, file with the clerk and serve on the appellant a designation of additional parts to be included.

(iii) The record on appeal consists of:

- the redesignated record as provided above;

- the proceedings in the district court or bankruptcy appellate panel; and

- a certified copy of the docket entries prepared by the clerk under Rule 3(d).

(C) *Forwarding the record.*

(i) When the record is complete, the district clerk or bankruptcy appellate panel clerk must number the documents constituting the record and send them promptly to the circuit clerk together with a list of the documents correspondingly numbered and reasonably identified. Unless directed to do so by a party or the circuit clerk, the clerk will not send to the court of appeals documents of unusual bulk or weight, physical exhibits other than documents, or other parts of the record designated for omission by local rule of the court of appeals. If the exhibits are unusually bulky or heavy, a party must arrange with the clerks in advance for their transportation and receipt.

(ii) All parties must do whatever else is necessary to enable the clerk to assemble and forward the record. The court of appeals may provide by rule or order that a certified copy of the docket entries be sent in place of the redesignated record, but any party may request at any time during the pendency of the appeal that the redesignated record be sent.

(D) *Filing the record.* Upon receiving the record or a certified copy of the docket entries sent in place of the redesignated record the circuit clerk must file it and immediately notify all parties of the filing date.

FRAP 7. BOND FOR COSTS ON APPEAL IN A CIVIL CASE

In a civil case, the district court may require an appellant to file a bond or provide other security in any form and amount necessary to ensure payment of costs on appeal. Rule 8(b) applies to a surety on a bond given under this rule.

FRAP 8. STAY OR INJUNCTION PENDING APPEAL

(a) *Motion for Stay.*

  (1) *Initial Motion in the District Court.* A party must ordinarily move first in the district court for the following relief:

   (A) a stay of the judgment or order of a district court pending appeal;

   (B) approval of a supersedeas bond; or

   (C) an order suspending, modifying, restoring, or granting an injunction while an appeal is pending.

  (2) *Motion in the Court of Appeals; Conditions on Relief.* A motion for the relief mentioned in Rule 8(a)(1) may be made to the court of appeals or to one of its judges.

   (A) The motion must:

    (i) show that moving first in the district court would be impracticable; or

    (ii) state that, a motion having been made, the district court denied the motion or failed to afford the relief requested and state any reasons given by the district court for its action.

   (B) The motion must also include:

    (i) the reasons for granting the relief requested and the facts relied on;

    (ii) originals or copies of affidavits or other sworn statements supporting facts subject to dispute; and

    (iii) relevant parts of the record.

   (C) The moving party must give reasonable notice of the motion to all parties.

   (D) A motion under this Rule 8(a)(2) must be filed with the circuit clerk and normally will be considered by a panel of the court. But in an exceptional case in which time requirements make that procedure impracticable, the motion may be made to and considered by a single judge.

(E) The court may condition relief on a party's filing a bond or other appropriate security in the district court.

(b) *Proceeding Against a Surety.* If a party gives security in the form of a bond or stipulation or other undertaking with one or more sureties, each surety submits to the jurisdiction of the district court and irrevocably appoints the district clerk as the surety s agent on whom any papers affecting the surety s liability on the bond or undertaking may be served. On motion, a surety's liability may be enforced in the district court without the necessity of an independent action. The motion and any notice that the district court prescribes may be served on the district clerk, who must promptly mail a copy to each surety whose address is known.

(c) *Stay in a Criminal Case.* Rule 38 of the Federal Rules of Criminal Procedure governs a stay in a criminal case.

FIFTH CIRCUIT RULE 8

Procedures in Death Penalty Cases Involving Applications for Immediate Stay of Execution and Appeals in Matters in Which the District Court Has Either Entered or Refused To Enter a Stay

8.1 Documents Required. Non-death penalty cases will be handled as described in FED. R. APP. P. 8. Death penalty cases arising from actions brought under 28 U.S.C. §§ 2254 and 2255 will be processed under the procedures found in this rule. The appellant must file 4 copies of the motion for stay and attach, to each, legible copies of the documents listed below. If the appellant asserts there is insufficient time to file a written motion, the appellant must deliver to the clerk 4 legible copies of each of the listed documents as soon as possible. If the appellant cannot attach or deliver any listed document, a statement why it cannot be provided must be substituted. The documents required are:

(a) The complaint or petition to the district court;

(b) Each brief or memorandum of authorities filed by both parties in the district court;

(c) The opinion giving the district court s reasons for denying relief;

(d) The district court judgment denying relief;

(e) The application to the district court for a stay;

(f) The district court order granting or denying a stay, and the statement of reasons for its action;

(g) The certificate of appealability or, if there is none, the order denying a certificate of appealability;

(h) A copy of each state or federal court opinion or judgment involving any issue presented to this court or, if the ruling was not made in a written opinion or judgment, a copy of the relevant portions of the transcript.

8.1.1 If the state indicates that it does not oppose the stay, and the applicant states this fact in the application, these documents do not need to be filed with the application but must be filed within 14 days after the application is filed.

8.1.2 If the appellant raises an issue that was not raised before the district court or has not been exhausted in state court, the applicant must give the reasons why prior action was not taken and why a stay should be granted.

__8.2 Panels.__ Death penalty case matters are handled by special panels selected in rotation from the court's regular screening panels. See 5TH CIR. R. 27.2.3 for handling applications for certificates of appealability.

__8.3 Motions To Vacate Stays.__ If the district court enters an order staying execution of a judgment, the party seeking to vacate the stay will attach 4 copies of each of the documents required by 5TH CIR. R. 8.1 to the motion.

__8.4 Emergency Motions.__ Emergency motions or applications, whether addressed to the court or to an individual judge, must be filed with the clerk rather than with an individual judge. If there is insufficient time to file a motion or application in person, by mail, or by fax, counsel may communicate with the clerk by telephone and thereafter must file the motion in writing with the clerk as soon as possible. The motion, application, or oral communication must contain a brief account of the prior actions of this or any other court or judge to which the motion or application, or a substantially similar or related petition for relief, was submitted.

__8.5 Merits.__ The parties must address the merits of each issue presented by an application. The panel may allow additional time to permit the parties adequate opportunity to do so.

__8.6 Consideration of Merits.__ If a certificate of appealability has been granted, the panel assigned to decide a motion for a stay of a state court judgment must, before denying a stay, consider and expressly rule on the merits of the appeal, unless the panel finds that the appeal is frivolous and entirely without merit.

8.7 Vacating Stays. *The panel assigned to an appeal must consider the merits before vacating a stay of execution, unless the panel rules the appeal is frivolous and entirely without merit.*

8.8 Mandate. *The panel may order the mandate issued instantly or after such time as it may fix.*

8.9 Stays of Execution Following Decision. *Stays to permit the filing and consideration of a petition for a writ of certiorari ordinarily will not be granted. The court must determine whether there is a reasonable probability that 4 members of the Supreme Court would consider the underlying issues sufficiently meritorious for the grant of certiorari and whether there is a substantial possibility of reversal of its decision, in addition to a likelihood that irreparable harm will result if its decision is not stayed.*

8.10 Time Requirements for Challenges to Death Sentences and/or Execution Procedures. *Inmates sentenced to death who wish to appeal an adverse judgment by the district court on a first petition for writ of habeas corpus, who seek permission to file a successive petition, or who seek to challenge their convictions, sentences, or the execution procedures (including but not limited to a suit filed pursuant to 42 U.S.C. § 1983), must exercise reasonable diligence in moving for a certificate of appealability, for permission to file a second or successive habeas petition, or in filing a notice of appeal from an adverse judgment of the district court in any other type of proceeding, and a stay of execution with the clerk of this court at least 7 days before the scheduled execution. Counsel who seek a certificate of appealability, permission to file a successive petition, or an appeal from a district court judgment less than 7 days before the scheduled execution must attach to the proposed filing a detailed explanation stating under oath the reason for the delay. If the motions are filed less than 7 days before the scheduled execution, the court may direct counsel to show good cause for the late filing. If counsel cannot do so, counsel will be subject to sanctions.*

If the state asks this court to vacate a district court order staying an execution, counsel for the state will file the state's appeal and application for relief from the stay as soon as practicable after the district court issues its order. Any unjustified delay by the state's counsel in seeking relief in this court will subject counsel to sanctions.

FRAP 9. RELEASE IN A CRIMINAL CASE

(a) *Release Before Judgment of Conviction.*

    (1) The district court must state in writing, or orally on the record, the reasons for an order regarding the release or detention of a defendant in a criminal case. A party appealing from the order must file with the court of appeals a copy of the district court's order and the court's statement of reasons as soon as practicable after filing the notice of appeal. An appellant who questions the factual basis for the district court's order must file a transcript of the release proceedings or an explanation of why a transcript was not obtained.

    (2) After reasonable notice to the appellee, the court of appeals must promptly determine the appeal on the basis of the papers, affidavits, and parts of the record that the parties present or the court requires. Unless the court so orders, briefs need not be filed.

    (3) The court of appeals or one of its judges may order the defendant's release pending the disposition of the appeal.

(b) *Release After Judgment of Conviction.* A party entitled to do so may obtain review of a district-court order regarding release after a judgment of conviction by filing a notice of appeal from that order in the district court, or by filing a motion in the court of appeals if the party has already filed a notice of appeal from the judgment of conviction. Both the order and the review are subject to Rule 9(a). The papers filed by the party seeking review must include a copy of the judgment of conviction.

(c) *Criteria for Release.* The court must make its decision regarding release in accordance with the applicable provisions of 18 U.S.C. §§ 3142, 3143, and 3145(c).

FIFTH CIRCUIT RULE 9

9.1 Release Before Judgment of Conviction. The clerk's office will advise counsel of the requirements of this rule after receiving a copy of a notice of appeal from the district court from an order respecting release entered prior to a judgment of conviction (FED. R. APP. P. 9(a)), or on counsel's advice a notice of appeal has been or will be filed.

Four copies of a memorandum must be filed within 10 days of the filing of the notice of appeal, clearly setting out the nature and circumstances of the offense charged and why the order respecting release is unsupported by the district court proceedings.

9.2 Release After Judgment of Conviction. *The original and 3 copies of an application regarding release pending appeal from a judgment of conviction (FED. R. APP. P. 9(b)) must be filed with the clerk of this court.*

(a) *The application for release must contain:*

(1) *The appellant's name;*

(2) *The district court docket number;*

(3) *The offense of which appellant was convicted; and*

(4) *The date and terms of sentence.*

(b) *The application must also contain:*

(1) *The legal basis for the contention that appellant is unlikely to flee or pose a danger to the safety of any other person or the community;*

(2) *An explanation why the district court's findings are clearly erroneous; and*

(3) *The issues to be raised on appeal that present substantial questions of law or fact likely to result in reversal or an order for a new trial on all counts of the indictment on which incarceration has been imposed, with pertinent legal argument establishing that the questions are substantial.*

9.3 Required Documents. *A copy of the district court's order respecting release pending trial or appeal, containing the written reasons for its ruling, must be appended to the memorandum or the application filed under 5TH CIR. R. 9.1 or 9.2.*

(a) *If the appellant questions the factual basis of the order, a transcript of the district court proceedings on the motion for release must be filed with this court. If the transcript is not filed with the memorandum or application, the appellant must attach a court reporter's certificate verifying that the transcript has been ordered and that satisfactory financial arrangements have been made to pay for it, together with the transcript's estimated date of completion.*

(b) *If the appellant cannot obtain a transcript of the proceedings, the appellant must state in an affidavit the reasons why not.*

9.4 Service. *A copy of the memorandum or application filed under 5TH CIR. R. 9.1 or 9.2 must be hand-delivered to government counsel or served by other expeditious method.*

9.5 Response. *The opposing party must file a written response to all requests for release within 10 days after service of the memorandum or application.*

FRAP 10. THE RECORD ON APPEAL

(a) *Composition of the Record on Appeal.* The following items constitute the record on appeal:

(1) the original papers and exhibits filed in the district court;

(2) the transcript of proceedings, if any; and

(3) a certified copy of the docket entries prepared by the district clerk.

(b) *The Transcript of Proceedings.*

(1) *Appellant's Duty to Order.* Within 14 days after filing the notice of appeal or entry of an order disposing of the last timely remaining motion of a type specified in Rule 4(a)(4)(A), whichever is later, the appellant must do either of the following:

(A) order from the reporter a transcript of such parts of the proceedings not already on file as the appellant considers necessary, subject to a local rule of the court of appeals and with the following qualifications:

(i) the order must be in writing;

(ii) if the cost of the transcript is to be paid by the United States under the Criminal Justice Act, the order must so state; and

(iii) the appellant must, within the same period, file a copy of the order with the district clerk; or

(B) file a certificate stating that no transcript will be ordered.

(2) *Unsupported Finding or Conclusion.* If the appellant intends to urge on appeal that a finding or conclusion is unsupported by the evidence or is contrary to the evidence, the appellant must include in the record a transcript of all evidence relevant to that finding or conclusion.

(3) *Partial Transcript.* Unless the entire transcript is ordered:

(A) the appellant must within the 14 days provided in Rule 10(b)(1) file a statement of the issues that the appellant intends to present on the appeal and must serve on the appellee a copy of both the order or certificate and the statement;

(B) if the appellee considers it necessary to have a transcript of other parts of the proceedings, the appellee must, within 14 days after the service of the order or certificate and the statement of the issues, file and serve on the appellant a designation of additional parts to be ordered; and

(C) unless within 14 days after service of that designation the appellant has ordered all such parts, and has so notified the appellee, the appellee may within the following 14 days either order the parts or move in the district court for an order requiring the appellant to do so.

(4) *Payment.* At the time of ordering, a party must make satisfactory arrangements with the reporter for paying the cost of the transcript.

(c) ***Statement of the Evidence When the Proceedings Were Not Recorded or When a Transcript Is Unavailable.*** If the transcript of a hearing or trial is unavailable, the appellant may prepare a statement of the evidence or proceedings from the best available means, including the appellant s recollection. The statement must be served on the appellee, who may serve objections or proposed amendments within 14 days after being served. The statement and any objections or proposed amendments must then be submitted to the district court for settlement and approval. As settled and approved, the statement must be included by the district clerk in the record on appeal.

(d) *Agreed Statement as the Record on Appeal.* In place of the record on appeal as defined in Rule 10(a), the parties may prepare, sign, and submit to the district court a statement of the case showing how the issues presented by the appeal arose and were decided in the district court. The statement must set forth only those facts averred and proved or sought to be proved that are essential to the court s resolution of the issues. If the statement is truthful, it together with any additions that the district court may consider necessary to a full presentation of the issues on appeal must be approved by the district court and must then be certified to the court of appeals as the record on appeal. The district clerk must then send it to the circuit clerk within the time provided by Rule 11. A copy of the agreed statement may be filed in place of the appendix required by Rule 30.

(e) *Correction or Modification of the Record.*

(1) If any difference arises about whether the record truly discloses what occurred in the district court, the difference must be submitted to and settled by that court and the record conformed accordingly.

(2) If anything material to either party is omitted from or misstated in the record by error or accident, the omission or misstatement may be corrected and a supplemental record may be certified and forwarded:

(A) on stipulation of the parties;

(B) by the district court before or after the record has been forwarded; or

(C) by the court of appeals.

(3) All other questions as to the form and content of the record must be presented to the court of appeals.

FIFTH CIRCUIT RULE 10

10.1 Appellant's Duty to Order the Transcript. The appellant's order of the transcript of proceedings, or parts thereof, contemplated by FED. R. APP. P. 10(b), must be on a form prescribed by the clerk. Counsel will furnish a copy of the order form to the clerk and to the other parties set out in FED. R. APP. P. 10(b). If no transcript needs to be ordered, appellant must file with the clerk a copy of a certificate to that effect that counsel served on the parties under FED. R. APP. P. 10(b).

10.2 Form of Record. The district court must furnish the record on appeal to this court in paper form, and in electronic form whenever available. The paper and electronic records on appeal must be consecutively numbered and paginated. The paper record must be bound in a manner that facilitates reading.

I.O.P. - THE DISTRICT COURT WILL FURNISH A TRANSCRIPT ORDER FORM, REQUIRED BY THIS COURT, WHEN THE NOTICE OF APPEAL IS FILED. ONCE COUNSEL COMPLETES THE TRANSCRIPT ORDER, FORWARDS IT TO THE REPORTER, AND MAKES ADEQUATE FINANCIAL ARRANGEMENTS, COUNSEL'S RESPONSIBILITY UNDER FED. R. APP. P. 10 AND 11 IS FULFILLED.

FRAP 11. FORWARDING THE RECORD

(a) *Appellant's Duty.* An appellant filing a notice of appeal must comply with Rule 10(b) and must do whatever else is necessary to enable the clerk to assemble and forward the record. If there are multiple appeals from a judgment or order, the clerk must forward a single record.

(b) *Duties of Reporter and District Clerk.*

    (1) *Reporter's Duty to Prepare and File a Transcript.* The reporter must prepare and file a transcript as follows:

        (A) Upon receiving an order for a transcript, the reporter must enter at the foot of the order the date of its receipt and the expected completion date and send a copy, so endorsed, to the circuit clerk.

        (B) If the transcript cannot be completed within 30 days of the reporter s receipt of the order, the reporter may request the circuit clerk to grant additional time to complete it. The clerk must note on the docket the action taken and notify the parties.

        (C) When a transcript is complete, the reporter must file it with the district clerk and notify the circuit clerk of the filing.

        (D) If the reporter fails to file the transcript on time, the circuit clerk must notify the district judge and do whatever else the court of appeals directs.

    (2) *District Clerk's Duty to Forward.* When the record is complete, the district clerk must number the documents constituting the record and send them promptly to the circuit clerk together with a list of the documents correspondingly numbered and reasonably identified. Unless directed to do so by a party or the circuit clerk, the district clerk will not send to the court of appeals documents of unusual bulk or weight, physical exhibits other than documents, or other parts of the record designated for omission by local rule of the court of appeals. If the exhibits are unusually bulky or heavy, a party must arrange with the clerks in advance for their transportation and receipt.

(c) *Retaining the Record Temporarily in the District Court for Use in Preparing the Appeal.* The parties may stipulate, or the district court on motion may order, that the district clerk retain the record temporarily for the parties to use in preparing the papers on appeal. In that event the district clerk must certify to the circuit clerk that the record on appeal is complete. Upon receipt of the appellee's brief, or earlier if the court orders or the parties agree, the appellant must request the district clerk to forward the record.

(d) *[Abrogated]*

(e) ***Retaining the Record by Court Order.***

(1) The court of appeals may, by order or local rule, provide that a certified copy of the docket entries be forwarded instead of the entire record. But a party may at any time during the appeal request that designated parts of the record be forwarded.

(2) The district court may order the record or some part of it retained if the court needs it while the appeal is pending, subject, however, to call by the court of appeals.

(3) If part or all of the record is ordered retained, the district clerk must send to the court of appeals a copy of the order and the docket entries together with the parts of the original record allowed by the district court and copies of any parts of the record designated by the parties.

(f) ***Retaining Parts of the Record in the District Court by Stipulation of the Parties.*** The parties may agree by written stipulation filed in the district court that designated parts of the record be retained in the district court subject to call by the court of appeals or request by a party. The parts of the record so designated remain a part of the record on appeal.

(g) ***Record for a Preliminary Motion in the Court of Appeals.*** If, before the record is forwarded, a party makes any of the following motions in the court of appeals:

- for dismissal;
- or release;
- for a stay pending appeal;
- for additional security on the bond on appeal or on a supersedeas bond; or
- for any other intermediate order

the district clerk must send the court of appeals any parts of the record designated by any party.

FIFTH CIRCUIT RULE 11

11.1 Duties of Court Reporters. *In all cases where transcripts are ordered, the court reporter must use a form provided by the clerk of this court and:*

(a) *Acknowledge receiving the transcript order, and indicate the date of receipt;*

(b) *State whether adequate financial arrangements have been made under the CJA, or otherwise;*

(c) Provide the number of trial or hearing days involved in the transcript, and estimate the total number of pages;

(d) Give an estimated date when the transcript will be finished; and

(e) Certify that he or she expects to file the transcript with the district court clerk within the time estimated.

11.2 Requests for Extensions of Time. *Court reporters seeking extensions of the time for filing the transcript beyond the 30 day period fixed by FED. R. APP. P. 11(b) must file an extension request with the clerk of this court and must specify in detail:*

(a) The amount of work accomplished on the transcript;

(b) A list of all outstanding transcripts due to this and other courts, including the due dates for filing; and

(c) A verification that the trial court judge who tried the case is aware of and approves the extension request.

If a court reporter's request for an extension of time is granted, he or she must promptly notify all counsel or unrepresented parties of the extended filing date and send a copy of the notification to this court.

11.3 Duty of the Clerk. *The district court clerk is responsible for determining when the record on appeal is complete for purposes of the appeal. Unless the record on appeal is sent to this court within 15 days from the filing of the notice of appeal or 15 days after the filing of the transcript of any trial proceedings, whichever is later, the district court clerk must advise the clerk of this court of the reasons for delay and request an extension to file the record. The clerk of this court may grant an extension for no more than 45 days. Extensions beyond 45 days are referred to a single judge. When transmitting the record on appeal in a direct criminal appeal involving more than one defendant, the district court must separate and identify the pleadings and any transcripts of pre-trial, sentencing, and post-trial hearings that apply to fewer than all of the defendants. However, only one copy of the trial transcript is required. In an action involving more than one defendant at trial but where separate actions are filed under 28 U.S.C. § 2255, the district court must separate and identify the pleadings and transcripts of pre-trial, sentencing, and post-trial hearings that apply to less than all of the defendants. One copy of the trial transcript is required for each defendant filing a separate § 2255 action.*

I.O.P. - THE CLERK WILL MONITOR ALL OUTSTANDING TRANSCRIPTS AND DELAYS.

ON OCTOBER 11, 1982, THE FIFTH CIRCUIT JUDICIAL COUNCIL ADOPTED A RESOLUTION REQUIRING EACH DISTRICT COURT IN THE FIFTH CIRCUIT TO DEVELOP A COURT REPORTER

MANAGEMENT PLAN PROVIDING FOR THE DAY-TO-DAY MANAGEMENT AND SUPERVISION OF AN EFFICIENT COURT REPORTING SERVICE WITHIN THE DISTRICT COURT. THESE PLANS MUST PROVIDE FOR THE SUPERVISION OF COURT REPORTERS IN THEIR RELATIONS WITH LITIGANTS AS SPECIFIED IN THE COURT REPORTER ACT, INCLUDING FEES CHARGED FOR TRANSCRIPTS, ADHERENCE TO TRANSCRIPT FORMAT PRESCRIPTIONS, AND DELIVERY SCHEDULES. THE PLANS MUST ALSO PROVIDE THAT A JUDGE, THE CLERK, OR SOME OTHER PERSON DESIGNATED BY THE COURT SUPERVISES THE COURT REPORTERS.

FRAP 12. DOCKETING THE APPEAL; FILING A REPRESENTATION STATEMENT; FILING THE RECORD

(a) *Docketing the Appeal.* Upon receiving the copy of the notice of appeal and the docket entries from the district clerk under Rule 3(d), the circuit clerk must docket the appeal under the title of the district-court action and must identify the appellant, adding the appellant s name if necessary.

(b) *Filing a Representation Statement.* Unless the court of appeals designates another time, the attorney who filed the notice of appeal must, within 14 days after filing the notice, file a statement with the circuit clerk naming the parties that the attorney represents on appeal.

(c) *Filing the Record, Partial Record, or Certificate.* Upon receiving the record, partial record, or district clerk s certificate as provided in Rule 11, the circuit clerk must file it and immediately notify all parties of the filing date.

FIFTH CIRCUIT RULE 12

Counsel can satisfy the representation statement required by FED. R. APP. P. 12(b) by completing this court s Notice of Appearance Form and returning it to the clerk within 30 days of filing the notice of appeal.

FRAP 12.1 REMAND AFTER AN INDICATIVE RULING BY THE DISTRICT COURT ON A MOTION FOR RELIEF THAT IS BARRED BY A PENDING APPEAL

(a) *Notice to the Court of Appeals.* If a timely motion is made in the district court for relief that it lacks authority to grant because of an appeal that has been docketed and is pending, the movant must promptly notify the circuit clerk if the district court states either that it would grant the motion or that the motion raises a substantial issue.

(b) *Remand After an Indicative Ruling.* If the district court states that it would grant the motion or that the motion raises a substantial issue, the court of appeals may remand for further proceedings but retains jurisdiction unless it expressly dismisses the appeal. If the court of appeals remands but retains jurisdiction, the parties must promptly notify the circuit clerk when the district court has decided the motion on remand.

TITLE III. REVIEW OF A DECISION OF THE UNITED STATES TAX COURT

FRAP 13. REVIEW OF A DECISION OF THE TAX COURT

(a) *How Obtained; Time for Filing Notice of Appeal.*

(1) Review of a decision of the United States Tax Court is commenced by filing a notice of appeal with the Tax Court clerk within 90 days after the entry of the Tax Court's decision. At the time of filing, the appellant must furnish the clerk with enough copies of the notice to enable the clerk to comply with Rule 3(d). If one party files a timely notice of appeal, any other party may file a notice of appeal within 120 days after the Tax Court s decision is entered.

(2) If, under Tax Court rules, a party makes a timely motion to vacate or revise the Tax Court's decision, the time to file a notice of appeal runs from the entry of the order disposing of the motion or from the entry of a new decision, whichever is later.

(b) *Notice of Appeal; How Filed.* The notice of appeal may be filed either at the Tax Court clerk s office in the District of Columbia or by mail addressed to the clerk. If sent by mail the notice is considered filed on the postmark date, subject to § 7502 of the Internal Revenue Code, as amended, and the applicable regulations.

(c) *Contents of the Notice of Appeal; Service; Effect of Filing and Service.* Rule 3 prescribes the contents of a notice of appeal, the manner of service, and the effect of its filing and service. Form 2 in the Appendix of Forms is a suggested form of a notice of appeal.

(d) *The Record on Appeal; Forwarding; Filing.*

(1) An appeal from the Tax Court is governed by the parts of Rules 10, 11, and 12 regarding the record on appeal from a district court, the time and manner of forwarding and filing, and the docketing in the court of appeals. References in those rules and in Rule 3 to the district court and district clerk are to be read as referring to the Tax Court and its clerk.

(2) If an appeal from a Tax Court decision is taken to more than one court of appeals, the original record must be sent to the court named in the first notice of appeal filed. In an appeal to any other court of appeals, the appellant must apply to that other court to make provision for the record.

FRAP 14. APPLICABILITY OF OTHER RULES TO THE REVIEW OF A TAX COURT DECISION

All provisions of these rules, except Rules 4-9, 15-20, and 22-23, apply to the review of a Tax Court decision.

TITLE IV. REVIEW OR ENFORCEMENT OF AN ORDER OF AN ADMINISTRATIVE AGENCY, BOARD, COMMISSION, OR OFFICER

FRAP 15. REVIEW OR ENFORCEMENT OF AN AGENCY ORDER — HOW OBTAINED; INTERVENTION

(a) *Petition for Review; Joint Petition.*

(1) Review of an agency order is commenced by filing, within the time prescribed by law, a petition for review with the clerk of a court of appeals authorized to review the agency order. If their interests make joinder practicable, two or more persons may join in a petition to the same court to review the same order.

(2) The petition must:

(A) name each party seeking review either in the caption or the body of the petition using such terms as et al., petitioners, or respondents does not effectively name the parties;

(B) name the agency as a respondent (even though not named in the petition, the United States is a respondent if required by statute); and

(C) specify the order or part thereof to be reviewed.

(3) Form 3 in the Appendix of Forms is a suggested form of a petition for review.

(4) In this rule "agency" includes an agency, board, commission, or officer; "petition for review includes a petition to enjoin, suspend, modify, or otherwise review, or a notice of appeal, whichever form is indicated by the applicable statute.

(b) *Application or Cross-Application to Enforce an Order; Answer; Default.*

(1) An application to enforce an agency order must be filed with the clerk of a court of appeals authorized to enforce the order. If a petition is filed to review an agency order that the court may enforce, a party opposing the petition may file a cross-application for enforcement.

(2) Within 21 days after the application for enforcement is filed, the respondent must serve on the applicant an answer to the application and file it with the clerk. If the respondent fails to answer in time, the court will enter judgment for the relief requested.

(3) The application must contain a concise statement of the proceedings in which the order was entered, the facts upon which venue is based, and the relief requested.

(c) ***Service of the Petition or Application.*** The circuit clerk must serve a copy of the petition for review, or an application or cross-application to enforce an agency order, on each respondent as prescribed by Rule 3(d), unless a different manner of service is prescribed by statute. At the time of filing, the petitioner must:

(1) serve, or have served, a copy on each party admitted to participate in the agency proceedings, except for the respondents;

(2) file with the clerk a list of those so served; and

(3) give the clerk enough copies of the petition or application to serve each respondent.

(d) ***Intervention.*** Unless a statute provides another method, a person who wants to intervene in a proceeding under this rule must file a motion for leave to intervene with the circuit clerk and serve a copy on all parties. The motion or other notice of intervention authorized by statute must be filed within 30 days after the petition for review is filed and must contain a concise statement of the interest of the moving party and the grounds for intervention.

(e) ***Payment of Fees.*** When filing any separate or joint petition for review in a court of appeals, the petitioner must pay the circuit clerk all required fees.

FIFTH CIRCUIT RULE 15

15.1 Docketing Fee and Copy of Orders - Agency Review Proceedings. At the time a party files a petition for review under FED. R. APP. P. 15, the party must:

(a) Pay the filing fee to the clerk; and

(b) Attach a copy of the order or orders to be reviewed.

15.2 Proceedings for Enforcement of Orders of the National Labor Relations Board. In National Labor Relations Board enforcement proceedings under FED. R. APP. P. 15(b), the respondent is considered the petitioner, and the board the respondent, for briefing and oral argument purposes, unless otherwise ordered by the court.

15.3 Proceedings for Review of Orders of the Federal Energy Regulatory Commission.

15.3.1 Petition for Review. Every petition for review must specify in its caption the number, date, and identification of the order reviewed and append the service list required by FED. R. APP. P. 15(c). Counsel filing the petition must attach a certificate that the commission has posted, filed or entered the order being reviewed.

   15.3.2 Docketing. All petitions for review and other documents concerning commission orders in the same number series (i.e., 699, 699A, 699B) are assigned to the same docket.

   15.3.3 Intervention.

(a) Party. A party to a commission proceeding may intervene in a review of the proceeding in this court by filing a notice of intervention. The notice must state whether the intervenor is a petitioner who objects to the order or a respondent who supports the order. A notice of intervention confers petitioner or respondent status on the intervening party as to all proceedings.

(b) Nonparty. A person who is not a party to a commission proceeding desiring to intervene in a review of that proceeding must file with the clerk, and serve upon all parties to the proceeding, a motion for leave to intervene. The motion must contain a concise statement of the moving party's interest, the grounds upon which intervention is sought, and why the interest asserted is not adequately protected by existing parties. Oppositions to such motions must be filed within 14 days of service.

   15.3.4 Docketing Statement. All parties filing petitions for review must file a joint docketing statement within 30 days of the filing of the initial petition for review, but not later than 14 days after the expiration of the period permitted for filing a petition for review. The docketing statement must:

(a) List each issue to be raised in the review;

(b) List any other pending review proceeding of the same order in any other court; and

(c) Attach copies of the order to be reviewed.

Every petitioner filing for review after filing a docketing statement must specify in the petition for review any exceptions taken or additions to the issues listed in the docketing statement. Every party who intervenes after the filing of the docketing statement must specify in the notice of intervention any exceptions taken to the issues listed in the docketing statement.

   15.3.5 Prehearing Conference. The clerk may give notice of a prehearing conference 10 days after filing of a docketing statement, or 14 days after entry of an order by the court deciding a venue issue, whichever is later. The prehearing conference will:

(a) Simplify and define issues;

(b) Agree on an appendix and record;

(c) Assign joint briefing responsibilities and schedule briefs; and

(d) Resolve any other matters aiding in the disposition of the proceeding.

Except for good cause, any party who petitions for review or intervenes after prehearing conference has been held is bound by the result of the prehearing conference.

15.3.6 Severance. Any petitioner or respondent may move to sever parties or issues by showing prejudice.

15.4 *Proceedings for Review of Orders of the Benefits Review Board.* *In petitions filed by either the claimant or the employer under 33 U.S.C. § 921 to review orders of the Benefits Review Board, the Office of Workers Compensation of the United States Department of Labor, the nominal respondent, is aligned with the claimant for briefing and oral argument purposes, unless otherwise ordered by the court. Within 30 days of the filing of the petition for review of the board's decision, the petitioner must file a statement of the issues to be presented on appeal and serve them on the director and counsel for all parties so the appropriate alignment can be made.*

15.5 *Time for Filing Motion for Intervention.* *A motion to intervene under* FED. R. APP. P. *15(d) should be filed promptly after the petition for review of the agency proceeding is filed, but not later than 14 days prior to the due date of the brief of the party supported by the intervenor.*

FRAP 15.1. BRIEFS AND ORAL ARGUMENT IN A NATIONAL LABOR RELATIONS BOARD PROCEEDING

In either an enforcement or a review proceeding, a party adverse to the National Labor Relations Board proceeds first on briefing and at oral argument, unless the court orders otherwise.

FRAP 16. THE RECORD ON REVIEW OR ENFORCEMENT

(a) *Composition of the Record.* The record on review or enforcement of an agency order consists of:

   (1) the order involved;

   (2) any findings or report on which it is based; and

   (3) the pleadings, evidence, and other parts of the proceedings before the agency.

(b) *Omissions From or Misstatements in the Record.* The parties may at any time, by stipulation, supply any omission from the record or correct a misstatement, or the court may so direct. If necessary, the court may direct that a supplemental record be prepared and filed.

FRAP 17. FILING THE RECORD

(a) *Agency to File; Time for Filing; Notice of Filing.* The agency must file the record with the circuit clerk within 40 days after being served with a petition for review, unless the statute authorizing review provides otherwise, or within 40 days after it files an application for enforcement unless the respondent fails to answer or the court orders otherwise. The court may shorten or extend the time to file the record. The clerk must notify all parties of the date when the record is filed.

(b) *Filing — What Constitutes.*

(1) The agency must file:

(A) the original or a certified copy of the entire record or parts designated by the parties; or

(B) a certified list adequately describing all documents, transcripts of testimony, exhibits, and other material constituting the record, or describing those parts designated by the parties.

(2) The parties may stipulate in writing that no record or certified list be filed. The date when the stipulation is filed with the circuit clerk is treated as the date when the record is filed.

(3) The agency must retain any portion of the record not filed with the clerk. All parts of the record retained by the agency are a part of the record on review for all purposes and, if the court or a party so requests, must be sent to the court regardless of any prior stipulation.

FIFTH CIRCUIT RULE 17

Filing of the Record. Any agency failing to file the record within 40 days, must request an extension of time and provide specific reasons justifying the delay. The clerk may grant an extension for no more than 30 days. After such an extension expires, the court may order production of the record.

FRAP 18. STAY PENDING REVIEW

(a) *Motion for a Stay.*

(1) *Initial Motion Before the Agency.* A petitioner must ordinarily move first before the agency for a stay pending review of its decision or order.

(2) *Motion in the Court of Appeals.* A motion for a stay may be made to the court of appeals or one of its judges.

(A) The motion must:

(i) show that moving first before the agency would be impracticable; or

(ii) state that, a motion having been made, the agency denied the motion or failed to afford the relief requested and state any reasons given by the agency for its action.

(B) The motion must also include:

(i) the reasons for granting the relief requested and the facts relied on;

(ii) originals or copies of affidavits or other sworn statements supporting facts subject to dispute; and

(iii) relevant parts of the record.

(C) The moving party must give reasonable notice of the motion to all parties.

(D) The motion must be filed with the circuit clerk and normally will be considered by a panel of the court. But in an exceptional case in which time requirements make that procedure impracticable, the motion may be made to and considered by a single judge.

(b) *Bond.* The court may condition relief on the filing of a bond or other appropriate security.

FRAP 19. SETTLEMENT OF A JUDGMENT ENFORCING AN AGENCY ORDER IN PART

When the court files an opinion directing entry of judgment enforcing the agency's order in part, the agency must within 14 days file with the clerk and serve on each other party a proposed judgment conforming to the opinion. A party who disagrees with the agency's proposed judgment must within 10 days file with the clerk and serve the agency with a proposed judgment that the party believes conforms to the opinion. The court will settle the judgment and direct entry without further hearing or argument.

FRAP 20. APPLICABILITY OF RULES TO THE REVIEW OR ENFORCEMENT OF AN AGENCY ORDER

All provisions of these rules, except Rules 3-14 and 22-23, apply to the review or enforcement of an agency order. In these rules, appellant includes a petitioner or applicant, and "appellee" includes a respondent.

TITLE V. EXTRAORDINARY WRITS

FRAP 21. WRITS OF MANDAMUS AND PROHIBITION, AND OTHER EXTRAORDINARY WRITS

(a) *Mandamus or Prohibition to a Court: Petition, Filing, Service, and Docketing.*

(1) A party petitioning for a writ of mandamus or prohibition directed to a court must file a petition with the circuit clerk with proof of service on all parties to the proceeding in the trial court. The party must also provide a copy to the trial-court judge. All parties to the proceeding in the trial court other than the petitioner are respondents for all purposes.

(2) (A) The petition must be titled In re [name of petitioner].

(B) The petition must state:

(i) the relief sought;

(ii) the issues presented;

(iii) the facts necessary to understand the issue presented by the petition; and

(iv) the reasons why the writ should issue.

(C) The petition must include a copy of any order or opinion or parts of the record that may be essential to understand the matters set forth in the petition.

(3) Upon receiving the prescribed docket fee, the clerk must docket the petition and submit it to the court.

(b) *Denial; Order Directing Answer; Briefs; Precedence.*

(1) The court may deny the petition without an answer. Otherwise, it must order the respondent, if any, to answer within a fixed time.

(2) The clerk must serve the order to respond on all persons directed to respond.

(3) Two or more respondents may answer jointly.

(4) The court of appeals may invite or order the trial-court judge to address the petition or may invite an amicus curiae to do so. The trial-court judge may request

permission to address the petition but may not do so unless invited or ordered to do so by the court of appeals.

(5) If briefing or oral argument is required, the clerk must advise the parties, and when appropriate, the trial-court judge or amicus curiae.

(6) The proceeding must be given preference over ordinary civil cases.

(7) The circuit clerk must send a copy of the final disposition to the trial-court judge.

(c) *Other Extraordinary Writs.* An application for an extraordinary writ other than one provided for in Rule 21(a) must be made by filing a petition with the circuit clerk with proof of service on the respondents. Proceedings on the application must conform, so far as is practicable, to the procedures prescribed in Rule 21(a) and (b).

(d) *Form of Papers; Number of Copies.* All papers must conform to Rule 32(c)(2). Except by the court s permission, a paper must not exceed 30 pages, exclusive of the disclosure statement, the proof of service, and the accompanying documents required by Rule 21(a)(2)(C). An original and 3 copies must be filed unless the court requires the filing of a different number by local rule or by order in a particular case.

FIFTH CIRCUIT RULE 21

Petition for Writ. The petition must contain a certificate of interested persons as described in 5TH CIR. R. 28.2.1. The certificate of interested persons and the items required by 5TH CIR. R. 21 do not count toward the page limit.

In addition to the items required by FED. R. APP. P. 21, the application must contain a copy of any memoranda or briefs filed in the district court supporting the application to that court for relief and any memoranda or briefs filed in opposition, as well as a transcript of any reasons the district court gave for its action.

I.O.P. MANDAMUS PROCESSING. IF THE PETITIONER DOES NOT ACCOMPANY THE PETITION WITH THE REQUISITE FILING FEE OR MOTION TO PROCEED IFP, THE CLERK WILL, BY LETTER, NOTIFY THE PETITIONER OF THE DEFECT AND SET A CORRECTION DEADLINE. IF THE PETITIONER FAILS TO MEET THE DEADLINE, THE CLERK WILL DISMISS THE PETITION 15 DAYS AFTER THE DEADLINE IN ACCORDANCE WITH OUR PRACTICES UNDER 5TH CIR. R. 42.3.1. IF THE PETITIONER ACCOMPANIES THE PETITION WITH THE REQUISITE FILING FEE OR MOTION TO PROCEED IFP, THE CLERK WILL DOCKET THE PETITION IN ACCORDANCE WITH FED. R. APP. 21(A)(3). WITH THE EXCEPTION OF AN EMERGENCY MANDAMUS PETITION, WHICH SHALL BE HANDLED IN ACCORDANCE WITH OUR EXISTING RULES FOR EMERGENCY MOTIONS, THE CLERK WILL FORWARD ALL MANDAMUS PETITIONS TO THE JURISDICTIONAL REVIEW CALENDAR OR A SCREENING PANEL FOR DISPOSITION.

TITLE VI. HABEAS CORPUS; PROCEEDINGS IN FORMA PAUPERIS

FRAP 22. HABEAS CORPUS AND SECTION 2255 PROCEEDINGS

(a) *Application for the Original Writ.* An application for a writ of habeas corpus must be made to the appropriate district court. If made to a circuit judge, the application must be transferred to the appropriate district court. If a district court denies an application made or transferred to it, renewal of the application before a circuit judge is not permitted. The applicant may, under 28 U.S.C. § 2253, appeal to the court of appeals from the district court's order denying the application.

(b) *Certificate of Appealability.*

(1) In a habeas corpus proceeding in which the detention complained of arises from process issued by a state court, or in a 28 U.S.C. § 2255 proceeding, the applicant cannot take an appeal unless a circuit justice or a circuit or district judge issues a certificate of appealability under 28 U.S.C. § 2253(c). If an applicant files a notice of appeal, the district clerk must send to the court of appeals the certificate (if any) and the statement described in Rule 11(a) of the Rules Governing Proceedings Under 28 U.S.C. § 2254 or § 2255 (if any), along with the notice of appeal and the file of the district-court proceedings. If the district judge has denied the certificate, the applicant may request a circuit judge to issue it.

(2) A request addressed to the court of appeals may be considered by a circuit judge or judges, as the court prescribes. If no express request for a certificate is filed, the notice of appeal constitutes a request addressed to the judges of the court of appeals.

(3) A certificate of appealability is not required when a state or its representative or the United States or its representative appeals.

FIFTH CIRCUIT RULE 22

Applications for Certificates of Appealability and Motions for Permission to File Second or Successive Habeas Corpus Applications. Applications for certificates of appealability, motions for permission to file second or successive applications under 28 U.S.C. §§ 2254 and 2255, and any responses must conform to the format requirements and the length limitations of FED. R. APP. P. 32(a), and 5TH CIR. R. 32 as applicable.

I.O.P. TO FED. R. APP. P. 22 - SEE 5TH CIR. R. 27.3 CONCERNING EMERGENCY MOTIONS. WHERE THE DISTRICT COURT HAS GRANTED A COA, THE CLERK SHALL INCLUDE IN THE ORIGINAL BRIEFING NOTICE A DEADLINE FOR ANY APPLICATION FOR COA ON ADDITIONAL ISSUES, AND WHERE FEASIBLE, SHALL MAKE THE DEADLINE COEXTENSIVE WITH THE BRIEFING DEADLINE.

FRAP 23. CUSTODY OR RELEASE OF A PRISONER IN A HABEAS CORPUS PROCEEDING

(a) *Transfer of Custody Pending Review.* Pending review of a decision in a habeas corpus proceeding commenced before a court, justice, or judge of the United States for the release of a prisoner, the person having custody of the prisoner must not transfer custody to another unless a transfer is directed in accordance with this rule. When, upon application, a custodian shows the need for a transfer, the court, justice, or judge rendering the decision under review may authorize the transfer and substitute the successor custodian as a party.

(b) *Detention or Release Pending Review of Decision Not to Release.* While a decision not to release a prisoner is under review, the court or judge rendering the decision, or the court of appeals, or the Supreme Court, or a judge or justice of either court, may order that the prisoner be:

   (1)   detained in the custody from which release is sought;

   (2)   detained in other appropriate custody; or

   (3)   released on personal recognizance, with or without surety.

(c) *Release Pending Review of Decision Ordering Release.* While a decision ordering the release of a prisoner is under review, the prisoner must   unless the court or judge rendering the decision, or the court of appeals, or the Supreme Court, or a judge or justice of either court orders otherwise   be released on personal recognizance, with or without surety.

(d) *Modification of the Initial Order on Custody.* An initial order governing the prisoner s custody or release, including any recognizance or surety, continues in effect pending review unless for special reasons shown to the court of appeals or the Supreme Court, or to a judge or justice of either court, the order is modified or an independent order regarding custody, release, or surety is issued.

   I.O.P. TO FED. R. APP. P. 23 - SEE 5TH CIR. R. 9.2 FOR PROCEDURES GOVERNING APPLICATIONS FOR RELEASE.

FRAP 24. PROCEEDING IN FORMA PAUPERIS

(a) *Leave to Proceed in Forma Pauperis.*

    (1) *Motion in the District Court.* Except as stated in Rule 24(a)(3), a party to a district-court action who desires to appeal in forma pauperis must file a motion in the district court. The party must attach an affidavit that:

        (A) shows in the detail prescribed by Form 4 of the Appendix of Forms the party's inability to pay or to give security for fees and costs;

        (B) claims an entitlement to redress; and

        (C) states the issues that the party intends to present on appeal.

    (2) *Action on the Motion.* If the district court grants the motion, the party may proceed on appeal without prepaying or giving security for fees and costs, unless a statute provides otherwise. If the district court denies the motion, it must state its reasons in writing.

    (3) *Prior Approval.* A party who was permitted to proceed in forma pauperis in the district-court action, or who was determined to be financially unable to obtain an adequate defense in a criminal case, may proceed on appeal in forma pauperis without further authorization, unless:

        (A) the district court before or after the notice of appeal is filed certifies that the appeal is not taken in good faith or finds that the party is not otherwise entitled to proceed in forma pauperis and states in writing its reasons for the certification or finding; or

        (B) a statute provides otherwise.

    (4) *Notice of District Court's Denial.* The district clerk must immediately notify the parties and the court of appeals when the district court does any of the following:

        (A) denies a motion to proceed on appeal in forma pauperis;

        (B) certifies that the appeal is not taken in good faith; or

        (C) finds that the party is not otherwise entitled to proceed in forma pauperis.

(5) ***Motion in the Court of Appeals.*** A party may file a motion to proceed on appeal in forma pauperis in the court of appeals within 30 days after service of the notice prescribed in Rule 24(a)(4). The motion must include a copy of the affidavit filed in the district court and the district court's statement of reasons for its action. If no affidavit was filed in the district court, the party must include the affidavit prescribed by Rule 24(a)(1).

(b) ***Leave to Proceed in Forma Pauperis on Appeal or Review of an Administrative-Agency Proceeding.*** When an appeal or review of a proceeding before an administrative agency, board, commission, or officer (including for the purpose of this rule the United States Tax Court) proceeds directly in a court of appeals, a party may file in the court of appeals a motion for leave to proceed on appeal in forma pauperis with an affidavit prescribed by Rule 24(a)(1).

(c) ***Leave to Use Original Record.*** A party allowed to proceed on appeal in forma pauperis may request that the appeal be heard on the original record without reproducing any part.

TITLE VII. GENERAL PROVISIONS

FRAP 25. FILING AND SERVICE

(a) *Filing.*

(1) *Filing with the Clerk.* A paper required or permitted to be filed in a court of appeals must be filed with the clerk.

(2) *Filing: Method and Timeliness.*

(A) *In general.* Filing may be accomplished by mail addressed to the clerk, but filing is not timely unless the clerk receives the papers within the time fixed for filing.

(B) *A brief or appendix.* A brief or appendix is timely filed, however, if on or before the last day for filing, it is:

(i) mailed to the clerk by First-Class Mail, or other class of mail that is at least as expeditious, postage prepaid; or

(ii) dispatched to a third-party commercial carrier for delivery to the clerk within 3 days.

(C) *Inmate filing.* A paper filed by an inmate confined in an institution is timely if deposited in the institution s internal mailing system on or before the last day for filing. If an institution has a system designed for legal mail, the inmate must use that system to receive the benefit of this rule. Timely filing may be shown by a declaration in compliance with 28 U.S.C. § 1746 or by a notarized statement, either of which must set forth the date of deposit and state that first-class postage has been prepaid.

(D) *Electronic filing.* A court of appeals may by local rule permit or require papers to be filed, signed, or verified by electronic means that are consistent with technical standards, if any, that the Judicial Conference of the United States establishes. A local rule may require filing by electronic means only if reasonable exceptions are allowed. A paper filed by electronic means in compliance with a local rule constitutes a written paper for the purpose of applying these rules.

(3) *Filing a Motion with a Judge.* If a motion requests relief that may be granted by a single judge, the judge may permit the motion to be filed with the judge; the judge must note the filing date on the motion and give it to the clerk.

(4) *Clerk's Refusal of Documents.* The clerk must not refuse to accept for filing any paper presented for that purpose solely because it is not presented in proper form as required by these rules or by any local rule or practice.

(5) *Privacy Protection.* An appeal in a case whose privacy protection was governed by Federal Rule of Bankruptcy Procedure 9037, Federal Rule of Civil Procedure 5.2, or Federal Rule of Criminal Procedure 49.1 is governed by the same rule on appeal. In all other proceedings, privacy protection is governed by Federal Rule of Civil Procedure 5.2, except that Federal Rule of Criminal Procedure 49.1 governs when an extraordinary writ is sought in a criminal case.

(b) *Service of All Papers Required.* Unless a rule requires service by the clerk, a party must, at or before the time of filing a paper, serve a copy on the other parties to the appeal or review. Service on a party represented by counsel must be made on the party s counsel.

(c) *Manner of Service.*

(1) Service may be any of the following:

(A) personal, including delivery to a responsible person at the office of counsel;

(B) by mail;

(C) by third-party commercial carrier for delivery within 3 days; or

(D) by electronic means, if the party being served consents in writing.

(2) If authorized by local rule, a party may use the court s transmission equipment to make electronic service under Rule 25(c)(1)(D).

(3) When reasonable considering such factors as the immediacy of the relief sought, distance, and cost, service on a party must be by a manner at least as expeditious as the manner used to file the paper with the court.

(4) Service by mail or by commercial carrier is complete on mailing or delivery to the carrier. Service by electronic means is complete on transmission, unless the party making service is notified that the paper was not received by the party served.

(d) *Proof of Service.*

(1) A paper presented for filing must contain either of the following:

(A) an acknowledgment of service by the person served; or

(B) proof of service consisting of a statement by the person who made service certifying:

(i) the date and manner of service;

(ii) the names of the persons served; and

(iii) their mail or electronic addresses, facsimile numbers, or the addresses of the places of delivery, as appropriate for the manner of service.

(2) When a brief or appendix is filed by mailing or dispatch in accordance with Rule 25(a)(2)(B), the proof of service must also state the date and manner by which the document was mailed or dispatched to the clerk.

(3) Proof of service may appear on or be affixed to the papers filed.

(e) *Number of Copies.* When these rules require the filing or furnishing of a number of copies, a court may require a different number by local rule or by order in a particular case.

FIFTH CIRCUIT RULE 25

25.1 Facsimile Filing. The clerk may accept, for filing, papers sent by facsimile in situations the clerk determines are emergencies or that present other compelling circumstances.

25.2 Electronic Case Filing Procedures.

25.2.1 Electronic Filing. At the court's direction, the clerk will set an implementation date for an initial period of voluntary, and a subsequent date for mandatory, use of the court's electronic filing system. Thereafter, all cases will be assigned to the court's electronic filing system. Counsel must register as Filing Users under Rule 25.2.3 and comply with the court's electronic filing standards, posted separately on the court's website, www.ca5.uscourts.gov, unless excused for good cause. Non-incarcerated pro se litigants may request the clerk's permission to register as a Filing User, in civil cases only, under such conditions as the clerk may authorize.

*Except as authorized in the electronic filing rules and standards, Filing Users must submit all briefs, motions, petitions for rehearing in PDF text, (not scanned), format **and** in paper format as prescribed by the clerk, see 5th Cir. R. 30, 31, etc. Whenever possible, other documents, e.g., record excerpts, etc., should be in PDF text format, and in paper format as prescribed by the clerk. All paper filings **must** be identical to the electronic file(s). Upon the clerk s request, a Filing User must promptly provide an identical electronic version of any paper document previously filed in the same case.*

25.2.2 Filings in Original Proceedings. Filing Users may be required to file case-initiating documents in original proceedings, e.g., mandamus, petitions for second and successive habeas corpus relief, petitions for review, etc., in paper format. Subsequent documents may be filed electronically and in paper format as prescribed by the clerk.

25.2.3 Filing Users: Eligibility, Registration, Passwords. All counsel not excused from filing electronically must register themselves, or any additional approved designee, as Filing Users of the court s electronic filing system. The clerk will define the registration requirements and continuing duty of counsel to keep their contact information current, see 5TH CIR. R. 46.1, and will determine necessary training to receive Filing User registration.

Non-incarcerated pro se litigants granted Filing User status under Rule 25.2.1 will have Filing User status terminated as prescribed by the clerk, generally at the termination of the case. If a pro se party, permitted to register as a Filing User, retains an attorney, that counsel must advise the clerk.

A Filing User s registration constitutes consent to electronic service of all documents as provided in the FED. R. APP. P. and the 5TH CIR. R.

Filing Users agree to protect the security of their passwords and immediately notify the PACER Service Center and the clerk if their password is compromised. Filing Users may be sanctioned for failure to comply with this provision.

Subject to a single judge s review, the clerk may terminate a Filing User s electronic filing privileges for abusing the system by an inordinate number of filings, filings of excessive size, or other failures to comply with the electronic filing rules and standards.

A Filing User may move to withdraw from participation in the electronic filing system for good cause shown.

25.2.4 Consequences of Electronic Filing. A Filing User s electronic transmission of a document to the electronic filing system consistent with these rules and the court s electronic filing standards, together with the court s transmission of a Notice of Docket Activity, constitutes filing of the document under the FED. R. APP. P. and 5TH CIR. R., and constitutes entry of the document on the docket under FED. R. APP. P. 36 and 45(b). If a party must file a motion for leave to file, both the motion and document at issue must be submitted electronically and in identical paper form; the underlying document will be filed if the court so directs.

A Filing User must verify a document s legibility and completeness before filing it with the court. Except as authorized by the court s electronic filing rules and standards, documents the Filing User creates and files electronically must be in PDF text format. When a Filing User s document has been filed electronically, the official record is the electronic document stored by the court, and the filing party is bound by the document as filed. Except for documents first filed in paper form and subsequently submitted electronically under 5TH CIR. R. 25.2.2, an electronically filed document is deemed filed at the date and time stated on the court s Notice of Docket Activity.

Filing must be completed by 11:59 p.m. Central Time to be considered timely filed that day.

25.2.5   Service of Documents by Electronic Means. The court s electronic Notice of Docket Activity constitutes service of the filed document on all Filing Users. Parties who are not Filing Users must be served with a copy of any document filed electronically in accordance with the FED. R. APP. P. 25 and 5TH CIR. R. 25 If the document is not available electronically, the filer must use an alternative method of service.

The court s electronic Notice of Docket Activity does not replace the certificate of service required by FED. R. APP. P. 25 (d).

25.2.6   Entry of Court - Issued Documents. Except as otherwise provided by rule or order, all of the court s orders, opinions, judgments, and proceedings relating to cases electronically filed will be filed in accordance with these rules, and will constitute entry on the docket under FED. R. APP. P. 36 and 45(b).

Any order or other court-issued document filed electronically does not require a signature of a judge or other court employee. An electronic order has the same force and effect as a paper copy of the order. Orders also may be entered as text-only entries on the docket, without an attached document. Such orders are official and binding.

25.2.7   Attachments and Exhibits to Motions and Original Proceedings. Filing Users must submit all documents referenced as exhibits or attachments, in electronic form within any file size limits the clerk may prescribe, as well as any paper copies the clerk specifies. A Filing User must submit as exhibits or attachments only those excerpts of the referenced documents that are directly germane to the matter under consideration by the court.

Excerpted material must be clearly and prominently identified as such. The clerk may require parties to file additional excerpts or the complete document.

25.2.8   Sealed Documents. A Filing User may move to file documents under seal in electronic form if permitted by law, and as authorized in the court's electronic filing standards. The court's order authorizing or denying the electronic filing of documents under seal may be filed electronically. Documents ordered placed under seal may be filed traditionally in paper or electronically, as authorized by the court. If filed traditionally, a paper copy of the authorizing order must be attached to the documents under seal and delivered to the clerk.

25.2.9   Retention Requirements. The Filing User must maintain in paper form documents filed electronically and requiring original signatures, other than that of the Filing User, for 3 years after the mandate or order closing the case issues. On request of the court, the Filing User must provide original documents for review.

25.2.10   Signatures. The user log-in and password required to submit documents in electronic form serve as the Filing User's signature on all electronic documents filed with the court. They also serve as a signature for purposes of the FED. R. APP. P. 32(d) and 5TH CIR. R. 28.5, and any other purpose for which a signature is required in connection with proceedings before the court.

The Filing User's name under whose log-in and password the document is submitted must be preceded by an "s/" and be typed in the space where the signature otherwise would appear.

No Filing User or other person may knowingly permit or cause to permit a Filing User's log-in and password to be used by anyone other than an authorized agent of the Filing User.

Documents which require more than one party's signature must be filed electronically by:

   submitting a scanned document containing all necessary signatures;

   showing the consent of the other parties on the document; or

   any other manner approved by the court.

Electronically represented signatures of all parties and Filing Users described above are presumed valid. If any party, counsel of record, or Filing User objects to the representation of his or her signature on an electronic document as described above, he or she must file a notice within 10 days setting forth the basis of the objection.

25.2.11 Notice of Court Orders and Judgment. The clerk will transmit electronically a Notice of Docket Activity to Filing Users in the case when entering an order or judgment. This electronic transmission constitutes the notice and service of the opinion required by FED. R. APP. P. 36(b) and 45(c). The clerk must give notice in paper form in accordance with those rules to a person who has not consented to electronic service.

25.2.12 Technical Failures. A Filing User whose filing is made untimely as the result of a technical failure may seek appropriate relief from the court.

25.2.13 Public Access/Redaction of Personal Identifiers. Parties must refrain from including, or must partially redact where inclusion is necessary, certain personal data identifiers whether filed electronically or in paper form as prescribed in FED. R. APP. P. 25, FED. R. CIV. P. 5.2(a), and FED. R. CRIM. P. 49.1. Responsibility for complying with the rules and redacting personal identifiers rests solely with counsel. The parties or their counsel may be required to certify compliance with these rules. The clerk will not review pleadings, and is not responsible for data redaction.

Parties wishing to file a document containing the personal data identifiers referenced above may:

file an un-redacted version of the document under seal, or

file a reference list under seal. The list must contain the complete personal data identifier(s) and the redacted identifier(s) used in its (their) place in the filing. All references in the case to the redacted identifiers included in the reference list will be construed to refer to the corresponding complete personal data identifier. The reference list must be filed under seal, and may be amended as of right.

The court will retain the un-redacted version of the document or the reference list as part of the record. The court may require the party to file a redacted copy for the public file.

25.2.14 Hyperlinks. Electronically filed documents may contain the following types of hyperlinks:

Hyperlinks to other portions of the same document;

Hyperlinks to PACER that contains a source document for a citation;

Hyperlinks to documents already filed in any CM/ECF database;

Hyperlinks between documents that will be filed together at the same time;

Hyperlinks that the clerk may approve in the future as technology advances.

Hyperlinks to cited authority may not replace standard citation format. Complete citations must be included in the text of the filed document. A hyperlink, or any site to which it refers, will not be considered part of the record. Hyperlinks are simply convenient mechanisms for accessing material cited in a filed document. The court accepts no responsibility for, and does not endorse, any product, organization, or content at any hyperlinked site, or at any site to which that site might be linked. The court accepts no responsibility for the availability or functionality of any hyperlink.

25.2.15 Changes. The clerk may make changes to the standards for electronic filing to adapt to changes in technology or to facilitate electronic filing. Changes to the court's electronic filing standards will be posted on the court's internet website.

I.O.P. - LIMITS ON RECOVERY OF MAILING OR COMMERCIAL CARRIER DELIVERY COSTS. SEE 5TH CIR. R. 39.2.

FRAP 26. COMPUTING AND EXTENDING TIME

(a) *Computing Time.* The following rules apply in computing any time period specified in these rules or in any local rule, court order, or in any statute that does not specify a method of computing time.

(1) **Period Stated in Days or a Longer Unit.** When the period is stated in days or a longer unit of time:

(A) exclude the day of the event that triggers the period;

(B) count every day, including intermediate Saturdays, Sundays, and legal holidays; and

(C) include the last day of the period, but if the last day is a Saturday, Sunday, or legal holiday, the period continues to run until the end of the next day that is not a Saturday, Sunday, or legal holiday.

(2) **Period Stated in Hours.** When the period is stated in hours:

(A) begin counting immediately on the occurrence of the event that triggers the period;

(B) count every hour, including hours during intermediate Saturdays, Sundays and legal holidays; and

(C) if the period would end on a Saturday, Sunday, or legal holiday, the period continues to run until the same time on the next day that is not a Saturday, Sunday, or legal holiday.

(3) **Inaccessibility of the Clerk's Office.** Unless the court orders otherwise, if the clerk s office is inaccessible:

(A) on the last day for filing under Rule 26(a)(1), then the time for filing is extended to the first accessible day that is not a Saturday, Sunday, or legal holiday; or

(B) during the last hour for filing under Rule 26(a)(2), then the time for filing is extended to the same time on the first accessible day that is not a Saturday, Sunday, or legal holiday.

(4) **"Last Day"Defined.** Unless a different time is set by statute, local rule, or court order, the last day ends:

    (A) for electronic filing in the district court, at midnight in the court's time zone;

    (B) for electronic filing in the court of appeals, at midnight in the time zone of the circuit clerk s principal office;

    (C) for filing under Rules 4(c)(1), 25(a)(2)(B), and 25 (a)(2)(C) and filing by mail under Rule 13(b) at the latest time for the method chosen for delivery to the post office, third-party commercial carrier, or prison mailing system; and

    (D) for filing by other means, when the clerk's office is scheduled to close.

(5) **"Next Day" Defined.** The next day is determined by continuing to count forward when the period is measured after an event and backward when measured before an event.

(6) **"Legal Holiday" Defined.** Legal Holiday means:

    (A) the day set aside by statute for observing New Year s Day, Martin Luther King Jr.'s Birthday, Washington's Birthday, Memorial Day, Independence Day, Labor Day, Columbus Day, Veterans Day, Thanksgiving Day or Christmas Day;

    (B) any day declared a holiday by the President or Congress; and

    (C) for periods that are measured after an event, any other day declared a holiday by the state where either of the following is located: the district court that rendered the challenged judgment or order, or the circuit clerk's principal office.

(b) *Extending Time.* For good cause, the court may extend the time prescribed by these rules or by its order to perform any act, or may permit an act to be done after that time expires. But the court may not extend the time to file:

    (1) a notice of appeal (except as authorized in Rule 4) or a petition for permission to appeal; or

(2) a notice of appeal from or a petition to enjoin, set aside, suspend, modify, enforce, or otherwise review an order of an administrative agency, board, commission, or officer of the United States, unless specifically authorized by law.

(c) *Additional Time after Service.* When a party may or must act within a specified time after service, 3 days are added after the period would otherwise expire under Rule 26(a), unless the paper is delivered on the date of service stated in the proof of service. For purposes of this Rule 26(c), a paper that is served electronically is not treated as delivered on the date of service stated in the proof of service.

FIFTH CIRCUIT RULE 26

26.1 Computing Time. Except for briefs and record excerpts, all other papers, including petitions for rehearing, are not timely unless the clerk actually receives them within the time fixed for filing. Briefs and record excerpts are deemed filed on the day sent to the clerk electronically where permitted by 5TH CIR. R. 30 and 31, by a third-party commercial carrier for delivery within 3 days, or on the day of mailing if the most expeditious form of delivery by mail is used. The additional 3 days after service by mail, by electronic means, or after delivery to a commercial carrier for delivery within 3 days referred to in FED. R. APP. P. 26(c), applies only to matters served by a party and not to filings with the clerk of such matters as petitions for rehearing under FED. R. APP. P. 40, petitions for rehearing en banc under FED. R. APP. P. 35, and bills of costs under FED. R. APP. P. 39.

26.2 Extensions of Time. The court requires timely filing of all papers within the time period allowed by the rules, without extensions of time, except for good cause. Appeals which are not processed timely will be dismissed for want of prosecution without further notice under 5TH CIR. R. 42. If the parties or counsel waive their right to file a reply brief, they must immediately notify the clerk to expedite submitting the case to the court.

FRAP 26.1. CORPORATE DISCLOSURE STATEMENT

(a) *Who Must File.* Any nongovernmental corporate party to a proceeding in a court of appeals must file a statement that identifies any parent corporation and any publicly held corporation that owns 10% or more of its stock or states that there is no such corporation.

(b) *Time for Filing; Supplemental Filing.* A party must file the Rule 26.1(a) statement with the principal brief or upon filing a motion, response, petition, or answer in the court of appeals, whichever occurs first, unless a local rule requires earlier filing. Even if the statement has already been filed, the party's principal brief must include the statement before the table of contents. A party must supplement its statement whenever the information that must be disclosed under Rule 26.1(a) changes.

(c) ***Number of Copies.*** If the Rule 26.1(a) statement is filed before the principal brief, or if a supplemental statement is filed, the party must file an original and 3 copies unless the court requires a different number by local rule or by order in a particular case.

FIFTH CIRCUIT RULE 26.1

26.1.1 Corporate Disclosure Statement. *The court uses a Certificate of Interested Persons in lieu of a Corporate Disclosure Statement. See* 5TH CIR. R. 28.2.1.

FRAP 27. MOTIONS

(a) *In General.*

(1) *Application for Relief.* An application for an order or other relief is made by motion unless these rules prescribe another form. A motion must be in writing unless the court permits otherwise.

(2) *Contents of a Motion.*

    (A) *Grounds and relief sought.* A motion must state with particularity the grounds for the motion, the relief sought, and the legal argument necessary to support it.

    (B) *Accompanying documents.*

        (i) Any affidavit or other paper necessary to support a motion must be served and filed with the motion.

        (ii) An affidavit must contain only factual information, not legal argument.

        (iii) A motion seeking substantive relief must include a copy of the trial court's opinion or agency's decision as a separate exhibit.

    (C) *Documents barred or not required.*

        (i) A separate brief supporting or responding to a motion must not be filed.

        (ii) A notice of motion is not required.

        (iii) A proposed order is not required.

(3) *Response.*

    (A) *Time to file.* Any party may file a response to a motion; Rule 27(a)(2) governs its contents. The response must be filed within 10 days after service of the motion unless the court shortens or extends the time. A motion authorized by Rules 8, 9, 18, or 41 may be granted before the 10-day period runs only if the court gives reasonable notice to the parties that it intends to act sooner.

    (B) *Request for affirmative relief.* A response may include a motion for affirmative relief. The time to respond to the new motion, and to reply to that response, are governed by Rule 27(a)(3)(A) and (a)(4). The title of the response must alert the court to the request for relief.

(4) *Reply to Response.* Any reply to a response must be filed within 7 days after service of the response. A reply must not present matters that do not relate to the response.

(b) *Disposition of a Motion for a Procedural Order.* The court may act on a motion for a procedural order including a motion under Rule 26(b) at any time without awaiting a response, and may, by rule or by order in a particular case, authorize its clerk to act on specified types of procedural motions. A party adversely affected by the court s, or the clerk's, action may file a motion to reconsider, vacate, or modify that action. Timely opposition filed after the motion is granted in whole or in part does not constitute a request to reconsider, vacate, or modify the disposition; a motion requesting that relief must be filed.

(c) *Power of a Single Judge to Entertain a Motion.* A circuit judge may act alone on any motion, but may not dismiss or otherwise determine an appeal or other proceeding. A court of appeals may provide by rule or by order in a particular case that only the court may act on any motion or class of motions. The court may review the action of a single judge.

(d) *Form of Papers; Page Limits; and Number of Copies.*

(1) *Format.*

(A) *Reproduction.* A motion, response, or reply may be reproduced by any process that yields a clear black image on light paper. The paper must be opaque and unglazed. Only one side of the paper may be used.

(B) *Cover.* A cover is not required, but there must be a caption that includes the case number, the name of the court, the title of the case, and a brief descriptive title indicating the purpose of the motion and identifying the party or parties for whom it is filed. If a cover is used, it must be white.

(C) *Binding.* The document must be bound in any manner that is secure, does not obscure the text, and permits the document to lie reasonably flat when open.

(D) *Paper size, line spacing, and margins.* The document must be on 8½ by 11 inch paper. The text must be double-spaced, but quotations more than two lines long may be indented and single-spaced. Headings and footnotes may be single-spaced. Margins must be at least one inch on all four sides. Page numbers may be placed in the margins, but no text may appear there.

(E) ***Typeface and type styles.*** The document must comply with the typeface requirements of Rule 32(a)(5) and the type-style requirements of Rule 32(a)(6).

(2) ***Page Limits.*** A motion or a response to a motion must not exceed 20 pages, exclusive of the corporate disclosure statement and accompanying documents authorized by Rule 27(a)(2)(B), unless the court permits or directs otherwise. A reply to a response must not exceed 10 pages.

(3) ***Number of Copies.*** An original and 3 copies must be filed unless the court requires a different number by local rule or by order in a particular case.

(e) ***Oral Argument.*** A motion will be decided without oral argument unless the court orders otherwise.

FIFTH CIRCUIT RULE 27

27.1 Clerk May Rule on Certain Motions. *Under* FED. R. APP. P. *27(b), the clerk has discretion to act on, in accordance with the standards set forth in the applicable rules, or to refer to the court, the procedural motions listed below. The clerk s action is subject to review by a single judge upon a motion for reconsideration made within the 14 or 45 day period set by* FED. R. APP. P. *40.*

27.1.1 To extend the time for: filing answers or replies to pending motions; paying filing fees; filing motions to proceed in forma pauperis; filing petitions for panel rehearing and rehearing en banc, and for reconsideration of single judge orders, for not longer than 14 days, 30 days if the applicant for extension is a prisoner proceeding pro se; filing briefs as permitted by 5TH CIR. R. *31.4; filing bills of costs; and filing applications under the Equal Access to Justice Act.*

27.1.2 To rule on motions to file briefs out of time.

27.1.3 To stay further proceedings in appeals.

27.1.4 To correct briefs or pleadings filed in this court at counsel s request.

27.1.5 To stay the issuance of mandates pending certiorari in civil cases only, for no more than 30 days, provided the court has not ordered the mandate issued earlier.

27.1.6 To reinstate appeals dismissed by the clerk.

27.1.7 To enter and issue consent decrees in labor board and other government agency review cases.

27.1.8 To enter CJA Form 20 orders continuing trial court appointment of counsel on appeal for purposes of compensation.

27.1.9 To consolidate appeals.

27.1.10 To withdraw appearances.

27.1.11 To supplement or correct records.

27.1.12 To incorporate records or briefs on former appeals.

27.1.13 To file reply or supplemental briefs in addition to the single reply brief permitted by FED. R. APP. P. 28(c) prior to submission to the court.

27.1.14 To file an amicus curiae brief under FED. R. APP. P. 29 (see 5TH CIR. R. 29.4).

27.1.15 To enlarge the number of pages of optional contents in record excerpts.

27.1.16 To extend the length limits for: briefs under FED. R. APP. P. 32(a)(7) and 5TH CIR. R. 32; petitions for rehearing en banc and panel rehearing under FED. R. APP. P. 35(b)(2), and 40(b); certificates of appealability and motions for permission to file second or successive habeas corpus applications under 28 U.S.C. §§ 2254 and 2255, under 5TH CIR. R. 22; petitions for permission to appeal under 5TH CIR. R. 5; and petitions for mandamus and extraordinary writs under 5TH CIR. R. 21.

27.1.17 To proceed in forma pauperis, see FED. R. APP. P. 24 and 28 U.S.C. § 1915.

27.1.18 To appoint counsel or to permit appointed counsel to withdraw.

27.1.19 To obtain transcripts at government expense.

27.2   Single Judge May Rule on Certain Motions. *Pursuant to FED. R. APP. P. 27(c), any single judge of this court has discretion, subject to review by a panel upon a motion for reconsideration made within the 14 or 45 day period set forth in FED. R. APP. P. 40, to take appropriate action on the following procedural motions:*

27.2.1   The motions listed in 5TH CIR. R. 27.1 that have been referred to a single judge for initial action, or for single judge reconsideration of a ruling made by the clerk, but the judge is not limited to the time restrictions in 5TH CIR. R. 27.1.1.

27.2.2   To permit interventions in agency proceedings pursuant to FED. R. APP. P. 15(d).

27.2.3 To act on applications for certificates of appealability under FED. R. APP. P. *22(b) and 28 U.S.C. § 2253 except for death penalty cases where a three judge panel must act.*

27.2.4 To extend for good cause the times prescribed by the Federal Rules of Appellate Procedure or by the rules of this court except for enlarging the time for initiating an appeal, see FED. R. APP. P. *26(b).*

27.2.5 To substitute parties under FED. R. APP. P. *43.*

27.2.6 To exercise the power granted in FED. R. APP. P. *8 and 9, respecting stays, or injunctions, or releases in criminal cases pending appeal, and subject to the restrictions set out in those rules; and to exercise the power granted in* FED. R. APP. P. *18, respecting stays pending review of agency decisions or orders, subject to the restrictions on the power of a single judge contained in that rule.*

27.2.7 To stay the issuance of mandates or to recall same pending certiorari.

27.2.8 To expedite appeals.

27.2.9 To strike a nonconforming brief or record excerpts as provided in 5TH CIR. R. *32.5 and to strike other papers not conforming to the* FED. R. APP. P. *and 5TH* CIR. R.

27.3 Emergency Motions in Cases Other Than Capital Cases. *Parties should not file motions seeking emergency relief unless there is an emergency sufficient to justify disruption of the normal appellate process. In cases not governed by 5th Cir. R. 8.10, motions seeking relief before the expiration of 14 days after filing must, subject to the penalties of* FED. R. APP. P. *46(c), be supported by good cause and must:*

Be preceded by a telephone call to the clerk's office and to the offices of opposing counsel advising of the intent to file the emergency motion. If time does not permit the filing of the motion by hand delivery or by mail, the clerk may permit filing by facsimile or by other electronic means. In an extraordinary case, the clerk may permit the submission of an oral motion by telephone. If the motion is filed by means other than hand delivery or mail, counsel should also later file the motion by hand delivery or by mail.

Be labeled "Emergency Motion."

State the nature of the emergency and the irreparable harm the movant will suffer if the motion is not granted.

Certify that the facts supporting emergency consideration of the motion are true and complete.

Provide the date by which action is believed to be necessary.
Attach any relevant order or other ruling of the district court as well as copies of all relevant

pleadings, briefs, memoranda, or other papers filed by all parties in the district court. If this cannot be done, counsel must state the reason that it cannot be done.
Be served on opposing counsel at the same time and, absent agreement to the contrary with

opposing counsel, in the same manner as the emergency motion is filed with the court.
Be filed in the clerk's office by 2:00 p.m. on the day of filing.

*27.3.1 Emergency Stays of Deportation. The court will give emergency consideration to stays of deportation **only** where the petitioner has a scheduled removal date and is in custody. Petitioners and counsel are responsible for obtaining accurate information about the custody status of their clients, as well as confirming the scheduled removal date. Emergency stays where petitioners have an imminent scheduled deportation date and are in custody will be processed in accordance with rule 27.3 above.*

***27.4** **Form of Motions.** Parties or counsel must comply with the requirements of FED. R. APP. P. 27 including the length limits of FED. R. APP. P.27(d)(2). Except for purely procedural matters, motions must include a certificate of interested persons as described in 5TH CIR. R. 28.2.1. Where a single judge or the clerk may act only an original and 1 copy need be filed. All motions requiring panel action require an original and 3 copies. **All motions must state that the movant has contacted or attempted to contact all other parties and must indicate whether an opposition will be filed.** Where a party's motion is not an Emergency Motion covered by 5th Cir. Rule 27.3, but the party has a serious need for the court to act within a specified time, the motion must state the time requirement and describe both the nature of the need and the facts that support it.*

***27.5** **Motions To Expedite Appeal.** Such motions are presented in the same manner as other motions. Only the court may expedite an appeal and only for good cause. If an appeal is expedited, the clerk will fix a briefing schedule unless a judge directs a specific date.*

I.O.P.

GENERAL STANDARDS FOR RULING ON MOTIONS

5TH CIR. R. 27 IMPLEMENTS FED. R. APP. P. 27(B) AND (C) AND DELEGATES TO SINGLE JUDGES AND THE CLERK THE AUTHORITY TO RULE ON SPECIFIED MOTIONS, SUBJECT TO REVIEW BY THE COURT. THIS I.O.P. PROVIDES THE GENERAL SENSE OF THE COURT ON THE DISPOSITION OF A VARIETY OF MATTERS:

BRIEFS - THE COURT EXPECTS THAT ALL BRIEFS WILL BE FILED TIMELY. MOTIONS FOR EXTENSION OF TIME TO FILE BRIEFS ARE DISFAVORED AND SHOULD BE MADE ONLY IN EXCEPTIONAL INSTANCES WHERE GOOD CAUSE EXISTS. NO EXTENSION IS AUTOMATIC. IF AN EXTENSION IS GRANTED, IT WILL BE FOR THE VERY LEAST AMOUNT OF TIME NECESSARY, AND EXCEPT IN THE MOST UNUSUALLY COMPELLING CIRCUMSTANCES, WILL NOT EXCEED 30 DAYS IN A CRIMINAL CASE, OR 40 DAYS IN A CIVIL CASE.

LITIGANTS SEEKING TO FILE BRIEFS AFTER THE DUE DATE SET IN THE BRIEFING LETTER SHOULD UNDERSTAND THAT THE COURT GENERALLY WILL NOT PERMIT THE BRIEF S FILING OUT OF TIME. HOWEVER EVEN IN THE UNUSUAL CASE WHERE OUT OF TIME FILING IS AUTHORIZED, A BRIEF GENERALLY WILL NOT BE FILED OUT OF TIME MORE THAN 30 DAYS BEYOND THE ORIGINAL DUE DATE IN A CRIMINAL CASE, OR 40 DAYS IN A CIVIL CASE.

MOTIONS FOR EXTENSION OF TIME TO FILE ANSWERS, REPLIES TO PENDING MOTIONS OR TO PAY FILING FEES - IF SUCH MOTIONS ARE GRANTED, EXTENSIONS GENERALLY WILL NOT EXCEED 30 DAYS.

REINSTATEMENT OF CASES DISMISSED BY THE CLERK - THE COURT NORMALLY WILL NOT REINSTATE A CASE DISMISSED BY THE CLERK UNDER 5TH CIR. R. 27.1.6 UNLESS:

THE DEFICIENCY WHICH CAUSED THE DISMISSAL HAS BEEN REMEDIED; AND

THE MOTION FOR REINSTATEMENT IS MADE AS SOON AS REASONABLY POSSIBLE AND IN ANY EVENT WITHIN 45 DAYS OF DISMISSAL.

MOTIONS PANELS - MOTIONS PANELS ARE DRAWN RANDOMLY FROM THE ACTIVE JUDGES. THESE PANELS ALSO OPERATE AS SCREENING PANELS AS DISCUSSED IN THE I.O.P. FOLLOWING 5TH CIR. R. 34. THE MOTIONS PANELS COMPOSITIONS ARE CHANGED AT THE BEGINNING OF EACH COURT YEAR TO PERMIT THE JUDGES TO SIT WITH OTHER JUDGES IN SCREENING AND HANDLING ADMINISTRATIVE MOTIONS.

DISTRIBUTION

TO JUDGES - MOTIONS REQUIRING JUDGES CONSIDERATION ARE ASSIGNED IN ROTATION TO ALL ACTIVE JUDGES ON A ROUTING LOG.

THE CLERK ASSEMBLES A COMPLETE SET OF THE MOTION PAPERS, AND ANY OTHER NECESSARY MATERIAL AND SUBMITS THEM WITH A ROUTING FORM TO THE INITIATING JUDGE. IN SINGLE JUDGE MATTERS THE JUDGE ACTS ON THE MOTION AND RETURNS IT TO THE CLERK WITH AN APPROPRIATE ORDER. FOR MOTIONS REQUIRING PANEL ACTION, A SINGLE SET OF PAPERS IS PREPARED, BUT THE INITIATING JUDGE TRANSMITS THE FILE TO THE NEXT JUDGE WITH A RECOMMENDATION. THE SECOND JUDGE SENDS IT ON TO THE THIRD JUDGE, WHO RETURNS THE FILE AND AN APPROPRIATE ORDER TO THE CLERK.

EMERGENCY MOTIONS - THE CLERK IMMEDIATELY ASSIGNS THE MATTER TO THE NEXT INITIATING JUDGE IN ROTATION ON THE ADMINISTRATIVE ROUTING LOG AND TO THE PANEL members. If the matter requires counsel to contact the initiating judge or panel members personally, the clerk will provide the names of the judges assigned the case, after getting approval from the initiating judge.

The motion papers are distributed as described above, except that a complete set, including any draft order, is forwarded to all members of the panel.

Motions After Assignment to Calendar - After cases are assigned to the oral argument calendar, motions are circulated to the hearing panel rather than to the standard motions panels. The senior active judge on the panel is considered the initiating judge. The clerk enters orders responding to the motions on behalf of the panel until entry of the opinion.

Post-Decision Motions

Extension of Time To File Petition for Rehearing or Leave To File Out of Time - The clerk may act on or refer to the court a timely motion for an extension of time to file a petition for panel rehearing or for rehearing en banc for a period not longer than 14 days, 30 days if the applicant is a prisoner proceeding pro se. Motions for additional time beyond 14 or 30 days, or to file out of time, are submitted to the writing judge, unless he or she is a visiting judge. In that event the matter is referred to the senior active judge on the panel. If the senior active judge dissented, the matter is referred to the other active judge on the panel.

Stay or Recall of Mandate - The clerk or a single judge, as appropriate, decides a motion for stay or recall of mandate pending action on a petition for writ of certiorari and routes and disposes of it in the same manner as in the preceding paragraph. (See 5th Cir. R. 27.1.5, 27.2.7, and 41).

Motions To Amend, Correct, or Settle the Judgment - These motions are referred to the writing judge with copies to the panel members.

Remand from Supreme Court of the United States - Remands from the Supreme Court of the United States are sent to the original panel for disposition when the Supreme Court's judgment is received. Counsel does not need to file a formal motion.

FRAP 28. BRIEFS

(a) *Appellant's Brief.* The appellant s brief must contain, under appropriate headings and in the order indicated:

(1) a corporate disclosure statement if required by Rule 26.1;

(2) a table of contents, with page references;

(3) a table of authorities cases (alphabetically arranged), statutes, and other authorities with references to the pages of the brief where they are cited;

(4) a jurisdictional statement, including:

    (A) the basis for the district court s or agency s subject-matter jurisdiction, with citations to applicable statutory provisions and stating relevant facts establishing jurisdiction;

    (B) the basis for the court of appeals jurisdiction, with citations to applicable statutory provisions and stating relevant facts establishing jurisdiction;

    (C) the filing dates establishing the timeliness of the appeal or petition for review; and

    (D) an assertion that the appeal is from a final order or judgment that disposes of all parties claims, or information establishing the court of appeals jurisdiction on some other basis;

(5) a statement of the issues presented for review;

(6) a statement of the case briefly indicating the nature of the case, the course of proceedings, and the disposition below;

(7) a statement of facts relevant to the issues submitted for review with appropriate references to the record (see Rule 28(e));

(8) a summary of the argument, which must contain a succinct, clear, and accurate statement of the arguments made in the body of the brief, and which must not merely repeat the argument headings;

(9) the argument, which must contain:

    (A) appellant s contentions and the reasons for them, with citations to the authorities and parts of the record on which the appellant relies; and

(B) for each issue, a concise statement of the applicable standard of review (which may appear in the discussion of the issue or under a separate heading placed before the discussion of the issues);

(10) a short conclusion stating the precise relief sought; and

(11) the certificate of compliance, if required by Rule 32(a)(7).

(b) *Appellee's Brief.* The appellee s brief must conform to the requirements of Rule 28(a)(1)-(9) and (11), except that none of the following need appear unless the appellee is dissatisfied with the appellant s statement:

(1) the jurisdictional statement;

(2) the statement of the issues;

(3) the statement of the case;

(4) the statement of the facts; and

(5) the statement of the standard of review.

(c) *Reply Brief.* The appellant may file a brief in reply to the appellee s brief. Unless the court permits, no further briefs may be filed. A reply brief must contain a table of contents, with page references, and a table of authorities cases (alphabetically arranged), statutes, and other authorities with references to the pages of the reply brief where they are cited.

(d) *References to Parties.* In briefs and at oral argument, counsel should minimize use of the terms appellant and appellee. To make briefs clear, counsel should use the parties' actual names or the designations used in the lower court or agency proceeding, or such descriptive terms as the employee, the injured person, the taxpayer, the ship," "the stevedore."

(e) *References to the Record.* References to the parts of the record contained in the appendix filed with the appellant s brief must be to the pages of the appendix. If the appendix is prepared after the briefs are filed, a party referring to the record must follow one of the methods detailed in Rule 30(c). If the original record is used under Rule 30(f) and is not consecutively paginated, or if the brief refers to an unreproduced part of the record, any reference must be to the page of the original document. For example:

• Answer p. 7;
• Motion for Judgment p. 2;

- Transcript p. 231.

Only clear abbreviations may be used. A party referring to evidence whose admissibility is in controversy must cite the pages of the appendix or of the transcript at which the evidence was identified, offered, and received or rejected.

(f) ***Reproduction of Statutes, Rules, Regulations, etc.*** If the court s determination of the issues presented requires the study of statutes, rules, regulations, etc., the relevant parts must be set out in the brief or in an addendum at the end, or may be supplied to the court in pamphlet form.

(g) *[Reserved]*

(h) *[Reserved]*

(i) ***Briefs in a Case Involving Multiple Appellants or Appellees.*** In a case involving more than one appellant or appellee, including consolidated cases, any number of appellants or appellees may join in a brief, and any party may adopt by reference a part of another's brief. Parties may also join in reply briefs.

(j) ***Citation of Supplemental Authorities.*** If pertinent and significant authorities come to a party s attention after the party s brief has been filed   or after oral argument but before decision   a party may promptly advise the circuit clerk by letter, with a copy to all other parties, setting forth the citations. The letter must state the reasons for the supplemental citations, referring either to the page of the brief or to a point argued orally. The body of the letter must not exceed 350 words. Any response must be made promptly and must be similarly limited.

FIFTH CIRCUIT RULE 28

28.1 ***Briefs - Technical Requirements.*** *The technical requirements for permissible typefaces, paper size, line spacing, and length of briefs are found in* FED. R. APP. P. *and* 5TH CIR. R. *32.*

28.2 ***Briefs - Contents.***

28.2.1 Certificate of Interested Persons. The certificate of interested persons required by this rule is broader in scope than the corporate disclosure statement contemplated in FED. R. APP. P. *26.1. The certificate of interested persons provides the court with additional information concerning parties whose participation in a case may raise a recusal issue. A separate corporate disclosure statement is not required. Counsel and unrepresented parties will furnish a certificate for all private (non-governmental) parties, both appellants and appellees, which must be incorporated on the first page of each brief before the table of contents or index, and which must certify a complete list of all persons, associations of persons, firms, partnerships, corporations, guarantors, insurers, affiliates, parent corporations, or other legal entities who or which are financially interested in the outcome of the litigation. If a large group of persons or firms can be specified by a generic description, individual listing is not necessary. Each certificate must also list the names of opposing law firms and/or counsel in the case. The certificate must include all information called for by FED. R. APP. P. 26.1(a). Counsel and unrepresented parties must supplement their certificates of interested persons whenever the information that must be disclosed changes.*

(a) *Each certificate must list all persons known to counsel to be interested, on all sides of the case, whether or not represented by counsel furnishing the certificate. Counsel has the burden to ascertain and certify the true facts to the court.*

(b) *The certificate must be in the following form:*

(1) *Number and Style of Case;*

(2) *The undersigned counsel of record certifies that the following listed persons and entities as described in the fourth sentence of Rule 28.2.1 have an interest in the outcome of this case. These representations are made in order that the judges of this court may evaluate possible disqualification or recusal.*
(*Here list names of all such persons and entities and identify their connection and interest.*)

Attorney of record for

28.2.2 Record References. Every assertion in briefs regarding matter in the record must be supported by a reference to the page number of the original record, whether in paper or electronic form, where the matter is found.

28.2.3 Request for Oral Argument. Counsel for appellant must include in a preamble to appellant's principal brief a short statement why oral argument would be helpful, or a statement that appellant waives oral argument. Appellee's counsel must likewise include in appellee's brief a statement why oral argument is or is not needed. The court will give these statements due, though not controlling, weight in determining whether to hold oral argument. See FED. R. APP. P. 34(a) and (f) and 5TH CIR. R. 34.2.

28.3 Brief - Order of Contents. *The order of contents of the brief is governed by* FED. R. APP. P. 28 *and this rule and will be as follows:*

(a) Certificate of interested persons required by 5TH CIR. R. 28.2.1;

(b) Statement regarding oral argument required by 5TH CIR. R. 28.2.3 (See FED. R. APP. P. 34(a)(1));

(c) A table of contents, with page references (see FED. R. APP. P. 28 (a)(2));

(d) A table of authorities (see FED. R. APP. P. 28(a)(3));

(e) A jurisdictional statement as required by FED. R. APP. P. 28(a)(4)(A) through (D);

(f) A statement of issues presented for review (see FED. R. APP. P. 28 (a)(5));

(g) A statement of the case (see FED. R. APP. P. 28(a)(6));

(h) A statement of facts relevant to the issues submitted for review (see FED. R. APP. P. 28(a)(7));

(i) A summary of the argument (see FED. R. APP. P. 28(a)(8));

(j) The argument (see FED. R. APP. P. 28(a)(9));

(k) A short conclusion stating the precise relief sought (see FED. R. APP. P. 28 (a)(10));

(l) A signature of counsel or a party as required by FED. R. APP. P. 32(d);

(m) A certificate of service in the form required by FED. R. APP. P. 25;

(n) A certificate of compliance if required by FED. R. APP. P. 32(a)(7) and 5TH CIR. R. 32.3.

28.4 Supplemental Briefs. *The rules do not permit the filing of supplemental briefs without leave of court, but there are some occasions, particularly after a case is orally argued or submitted on the summary calendar, where the court will call for supplemental briefs on particular issues. Also, where intervening decisions or new developments should be brought to the court's attention, counsel may direct a letter, not a supplemental brief, to the clerk with citations and succinct comment. See FED. R. APP. P. 28(j). If a new case is not reported, copies of the decision should be appended. The letter must be filed in 4 copies, and served on opposing counsel.*

28.5 Signing the Brief. *See FED. R. APP. P. 32(d). The signature requirement is interpreted broadly, and the attorney of record may designate another person to sign the brief for him or her. Where counsel for a particular party reside in different locations, it is not* *necessary to incur the expense of sending the brief from one person to another for multiple signatures.*

28.6 Pro Se Briefs. *Unless specifically directed by court order, pro se motions, briefs or correspondence will not be filed if the party is represented by counsel.*

28.7 Citation to Unpublished Opinions, Orders, etc. *FED. R. APP. P. 32.1(a) permits citation to unpublished judicial dispositions. Parties citing to such dispositions must comply with FED. R. APP. P. 32.1(b). If a party does not need to submit a copy of an unpublished disposition, the party must provide a citation to the disposition in a publicly accessible electronic database.*

I.O.P. - MISCELLANEOUS BRIEF INFORMATION

(A) ACKNOWLEDGMENT OF BRIEFS - THE CLERK DOES NOT ACKNOWLEDGE THE FILING OF BRIEFS UNLESS COUNSEL OR A PARTY MAKES A SPECIAL REQUEST.

(B) SAMPLE BRIEFS AND RECORD EXCERPTS - UPON REQUEST, THE CLERK MAY LOAN SAMPLE BRIEFS AND RECORD EXCERPTS TO COUNSEL AND NON-INCARCERATED PRO SE LITIGANTS. BECAUSE PRO SE PRISONER BRIEFS ARE NOT HELD TO THE SAME RIGID STANDARDS AS OTHER BRIEFS, COPIES OF BRIEFS ARE GENERALLY NOT SENT TO PRISONERS. INSTEAD OTHER INFORMATIONAL MATERIAL MAY BE SENT. POSTAGE FEES MAY BE REQUIRED BEFORE THE MATERIALS ARE SENT.

(C) CHECKLIST AVAILABLE - A COPY OF THE CHECKLIST USED BY THE CLERK IN EXAMINING BRIEFS IS AVAILABLE ON REQUEST.

FRAP 28.1   CROSS-APPEALS

(a) ***Applicability.*** This rules applies to a case in which a cross-appeal is filed. Rules 28(a)-(c), 31(a)(1), 32(a)(2), and 32(a)(7)(A)-(B) do not apply to such a case, except as otherwise provided in this rule.

(b) ***Designation of Appellant.*** The party who files a notice of appeal first is the appellant for the purposes of this rule and Rules 30 and 34. If notices are filed on the same day, the plaintiff in the proceeding below is the appellant. These designations may be modified by the parties agreement or by court order.

(c) ***Briefs.*** In a case involving a cross-appeal:

(1) ***Appellant's Principal Brief.*** The appellant must file a principal brief in the appeal. That brief must comply with Rule 28(a).

(2) ***Appellee's Principal and Response Brief.*** The appellee must file a principal brief in the cross-appeal and must, in the same brief, respond to the principal brief in the appeal. That appellee s brief must comply with Rule 28(a), except that the brief need not include a statement of the case or a statement of the facts unless the appellee is dissatisfied with the appellant s statement.

(3) ***Appellant's Response and Reply Brief.*** The appellant must file a brief that responds to the principal brief in the cross-appeal and may, in the same brief, reply to the response in the appeal. That brief must comply with Rule 28(a)(2)-(9) and (11), except that none of the following need appear unless the appellant is dissatisfied with the appellee's statement in the cross-appeal:

(A) the jurisdictional statement;

(B) the statement of the issues;

(C) the statement of the case;

(D) the statement of the facts; and

(E) the statement of the standard of review.

(4) ***Appellee's Reply Brief.*** The appellee may file a brief in reply to the response in the cross-appeal. That brief must comply with Rule 28(a)(2)-(3) and (11) and must be limited to the issues presented by the cross-appeal.

(5) ***No Further Briefs.*** Unless the court permits, no further briefs may be filed in a case involving a cross-appeal.

(d) *Cover.* Except for filings by unrepresented parties, the cover of the appellant's principal brief must be blue; the appellee s principal and response brief, red; the appellant s response and reply brief, yellow; the appellee's reply brief, gray; an intervenor's or amicus curiae s brief, green; and any supplemental brief, tan. The front cover of a brief must contain the information required by Rule 32(a)(2).

(e) *Length.*

(1) ***Page Limitation.*** Unless it complies with Rule 28.1(e)(2) and (3), the appellant s principal brief must not exceed 30 pages; the appellee's principal and response brief, 35 pages; the appellant s response and reply brief, 30 pages; and the appellee s reply brief, 15 pages.

(2) *Type-Volume Limitation.*

 (A) The appellant s principal brief or the appellant s response and reply brief is acceptable if:

  (i) it contains no more that 14,000 words; or

  (ii) it uses a monospaced face and contains no more than 1,300 lines of text.

 (B) The appellee s principal and response brief is acceptable if:

  (i) it contains no more than 16,500 words; or

  (ii) it uses a monospaced face and contains no more than 1,500 lines of text.

 (C) The appellee s reply brief is acceptable if it contains no more than half of the type volume specified in Rule 28.1(e)(2)(A).

(3) *Certificate of Compliance.* A brief submitted under Rule 28.1(e)(2) must comply with Rule 32(a)(7)(C).

(f) *Time to Serve and File a Brief.* Briefs must be served and filed as follows:

(1) the appellant's principal brief, within 40 days after the record is filed;

(2) the appellee's principal and response brief, within 30 days after the appellant's principal brief is served;

(3) the appellant s response and reply brief, within 30 days after the appellee s principal and response brief is served; and

(4) the appellee's reply brief, within 14 days after the appellant's response and reply brief is served, but at least 7 days before argument unless the court, for good cause, allows a later filing.

FRAP 29. BRIEF OF AN AMICUS CURIAE

(a) *When Permitted.* The United States or its officer or agency, or a state may file an amicus-curiae brief without the consent of the parties or leave of court. Any other amicus curiae may file a brief only by leave of court or if the brief states that all parties have consented to its filing.

(b) *Motion for Leave to File.* The motion must be accompanied by the proposed brief and state:

(1) the movant's interest; and

(2) the reason why an amicus brief is desirable and why the matters asserted are relevant to the disposition of the case.

(c) *Contents and Form.* An amicus brief must comply with Rule 32. In addition to the requirements of Rule 32, the cover must identify the party or parties supported and indicate whether the brief supports affirmance or reversal. An amicus brief need not comply with Rule 28, but must include the following:

(1) if the amicus curiae is a corporation, a disclosure statement like that required of parties by Rule 26.1;

(2) a table of contents, with page references;

(3) a table of authorities — cases (alphabetically arranged), statutes and other authorities — with references to the pages of the brief where they are cited;

(4) a concise statement of the identity of the amicus curiae, its interest in the case, and the source of its authority to file;

(5) unless the amicus curiae is one listed in the first sentence of Rule 29(a), a statement that indicates whether:

(A) a party's counsel authored the brief in whole or in part;

(B) a party or a party's counsel contributed money that was intended to fund preparing or submitting the brief;

(C) a person — other than the amicus curiae, its members, or its counsel — contributed money that was intended to fund preparing or submitting the brief and, if so identifies each such person;

(6) argument, which may be preceded by a summary and which need not include a statement of the applicable standard of review; and

(7) a certificate of compliance, if required by Rule 32(a)(7).

(d) *Length.* Except by the court's permission, an amicus brief may be no more than one-half the maximum length authorized by these rules for a party s principal brief. If the court grants a party permission to file a longer brief, that extension does not affect the length of an amicus brief.

(e) *Time for Filing.* An amicus curiae must file its brief, accompanied by a motion for filing when necessary, no later than 7 days after the principal brief of the party being supported is filed. An amicus curiae that does not support either party must file its brief no later than 7 days after the appellant's or petitioner's principal brief is filed. A court may grant leave for later filing, specifying the time within which an opposing party may answer.

(f) *Reply Brief.* Except by the court's permission, an amicus curiae may not file a reply brief.

(g) *Oral Argument.* An amicus curiae may participate in oral argument only with the court s permission.

FIFTH CIRCUIT RULE 29

29.1 *Time for Filing Motion. Those wishing to file an amicus curiae brief should file a motion within 7 days after the filing of the principal brief of the party whose position the amicus brief will support.*

29.2 *Contents and Form. Briefs filed under this rule must comply with the applicable FED. R. APP. P. provisions and with 5TH CIR. R. 31 and 32. The brief must include a supplemental statement of interested parties, if necessary to fully disclose all those with an interest in the amicus brief. The brief should avoid the repetition of facts or legal arguments contained in the principal brief and should focus on points either not made or not adequately discussed in those briefs. Any non-conforming brief may be stricken, on motion or sua sponte.*

29.3 *Length of Briefs. See FED. R. APP. P. 29(d).*

29.4 *Denial of Amicus Curiae Status. After a panel opinion is issued, amicus curiae status will not be permitted if the allowance would result in the disqualification of any member of the panel or of the en banc court.*

I.O.P. - SEE ALSO 5TH CIR. R. 31.2 .

FRAP 30. APPENDIX TO THE BRIEFS

(a) *Appellant's Responsibility.*

(1) *Contents of the Appendix.* The appellant must prepare and file an appendix to the briefs containing:

   (A) the relevant docket entries in the proceeding below;

   (B) the relevant portions of the pleadings, charge, findings, or opinion;

   (C) the judgment, order, or decision in question; and

   (D) other parts of the record to which the parties wish to direct the court s attention.

(2) *Excluded Material.* Memoranda of law in the district court should not be included in the appendix unless they have independent relevance. Parts of the record may be relied on by the court or the parties even though not included in the appendix.

(3) *Time to File; Number of Copies.* Unless filing is deferred under Rule 30(c), the appellant must file 10 copies of the appendix with the brief and must serve one copy on counsel for each party separately represented. An unrepresented party proceeding in forma pauperis must file 4 legible copies with the clerk, and one copy must be served on counsel for each separately represented party. The court may by local rule or by order in a particular case require the filing or service of a different number.

(b) *All Parties' Responsibilities.*

(1) *Determining the Contents of the Appendix.* The parties are encouraged to agree on the contents of the appendix. In the absence of an agreement, the appellant must, within 14 days after the record is filed, serve on the appellee a designation of the parts of the record the appellant intends to include in the appendix and a statement of the issues the appellant intends to present for review. The appellee may, within 14 days after receiving the designation, serve on the appellant a designation of additional parts to which it wishes to direct the court s attention. The appellant must include the designated parts in the appendix. The parties must not engage in unnecessary designation of parts of the record, because the entire record is available to the court. This paragraph applies also to a cross-appellant and a cross-appellee.

(2) *Costs of Appendix.* Unless the parties agree otherwise, the appellant must pay the cost of the appendix. If the appellant considers parts of the record designated by the appellee to be unnecessary, the appellant may advise the appellee, who must then advance the cost

of including those parts. The cost of the appendix is a taxable cost. But if any party causes unnecessary parts of the record to be included in the appendix, the court may impose the cost of those parts on that party. Each circuit must, by local rule, provide for sanctions against attorneys who unreasonably and vexatiously increase litigation costs by including unnecessary material in the appendix.

(c) *Deferred Appendix.*

(1) *Deferral Until After Briefs Are Filed.* The court may provide by rule for classes of cases or by order in a particular case that preparation of the appendix may be deferred until after the briefs have been filed and that the appendix may be filed 21 days after the appellee s brief is served. Even though the filing of the appendix may be deferred, Rule 30(b) applies; except that a party must designate the parts of the record it wants included in the appendix when it serves its brief, and need not include a statement of the issues presented.

(2) *References to the Record.*

(A) If the deferred appendix is used, the parties may cite in their briefs the pertinent pages of the record. When the appendix is prepared, the record pages cited in the briefs must be indicated by inserting record page numbers, in brackets, at places in the appendix where those pages of the record appear.

(B) A party who wants to refer directly to pages of the appendix may serve and file copies of the brief within the time required by Rule 31(a), containing appropriate references to pertinent pages of the record. In that event, within 14 days after the appendix is filed, the party must serve and file copies of the brief, containing references to the pages of the appendix in place of or in addition to the references to the pertinent pages of the record. Except for the correction of typographical errors, no other changes may be made to the brief.

(d) *Format of the Appendix.* The appendix must begin with a table of contents identifying the page at which each part begins. The relevant docket entries must follow the table of contents. Other parts of the record must follow chronologically. When pages from the transcript of proceedings are placed in the appendix, the transcript page numbers must be shown in brackets immediately before the included pages. Omissions in the text of papers or of the transcript must be indicated by asterisks. Immaterial formal matters (captions, subscriptions, acknowledgments, etc.) should be omitted.

(e) *Reproduction of Exhibits.* Exhibits designated for inclusion in the appendix may be reproduced in a separate volume, or volumes, suitably indexed. Four copies must be filed with the appendix, and one copy must be served on counsel for each separately represented party. If a transcript of a proceeding before an administrative agency, board, commission, or officer was used in a district-court action and has been designated for inclusion in the appendix, the transcript must be placed in the appendix as an exhibit.

(f) *Appeal on the Original Record Without an Appendix.* The court may, either by rule for all cases or classes of cases or by order in a particular case, dispense with the appendix and permit an appeal to proceed on the original record with any copies of the record, or relevant parts, that the court may order the parties to file.

FIFTH CIRCUIT RULE 30

30.1 Records on Appeal/Record Excerpts/Appendix - Appeals from District Courts, the Tax Court, and Agencies. Appeals from district courts and the Tax Court are decided on the original record on appeal (ROA). The clerk is authorized to require the party receiving the ROA to pay reasonable shipping costs as a condition of receiving the record. Moreover, counsel and unrepresented parties must review the ROA within 20 days of dispatch from the clerk's office and advise electronically or in writing both the appropriate District Court (or the Tax Court, if appropriate) and Fifth Circuit clerk's offices of any errors in, or omissions from, the ROA. Failure to comply may result in a denial of any requested extension of time to file a brief due to an alleged error in, or incomplete ROA. Record excerpts are filed in lieu of the appendix prescribed by FED. R. APP. P. 30. Petitions for review or enforcement of agency orders are governed by 5TH CIR. R. 30.2, but parties may be required to pay reasonable shipping costs, and are responsible for timely review of the record and the notification requirements set out above.

30.1.1 Purpose. The record excerpts are intended primarily to assist the judges in making the screening decision on the need for oral argument and in preparing for oral argument. Counsel need excerpt only those parts of the record that will assist in these functions.

30.1.2 Filing. Four paper copies of excerpts of the district court record must accompany the appellant's brief, see 5TH CIR. R. 30.1.4 and 30.1.5. If exempt from electronic filing under 5TH CIR. R. 25.2, all appellants represented by counsel must file an electronic copy of the record excerpts on a CD, computer diskette, or such other electronic medium as the clerk may authorize. The electronic copy must be in a single Portable Document Format (PDF) file; contain nothing other than the record excerpts; and have as the first page of the electronic copy an index to the contents. If submitted on a CD, diskette, or other authorized physical media, the electronic version must have a label containing the case name and docket number and state Record Excerpts. The appellant must serve a paper and electronic copy of the excerpts on counsel for each of the parties separately represented; a paper copy on any party proceeding pro se, and an electronic copy, if the pro se party is not an inmate confined in an institution. The appellee may similarly submit and serve additional record excerpts with the appellee s principal brief, with the required copies furnished to the clerk accompanying the appellee s brief.

30.1.3 Prisoner Petitions Without Representation by Counsel. Prisoners without counsel are not required to prepare and file record excerpts.

30.1.4 Mandatory Contents. The record excerpts must contain copies of the following portions of the district court record:

(a) *The docket sheet;*

(b) *The notice of appeal;*

(c) *The indictment in criminal cases;*

(d) *The jury s verdict in all cases;*

(e) *The judgment or interlocutory order appealed;*

(f) *Any other orders or rulings sought to be reviewed;*

(g) *Any relevant magistrate judge s report and recommendation;*

(h) *Any supporting opinion or findings of fact and conclusions of law filed, or transcript pages of any such delivered orally; and*

(i) *A certificate of service complying with FED. R. APP. P. 25.*

30.1.5 Optional Contents. The record excerpts may include those parts of the record, referred to in the briefs including:

(a) *Essential pleadings or relevant portions thereof;*

(b) *The parts of the FED. R. CIV. P. 16(e) pretrial order relevant to any issue on appeal;*

(c) *Any jury instruction given or refused that presents an issue on appeal, together with any objection and the court's ruling, and any other relevant part of the jury charge;*

(d) *Findings and conclusions of the administrative law judge, if the appeal is of a court order reviewing an administrative agency determination;*

(e) A copy of the relevant pages of the transcript when the appeal challenges the admission or exclusion of evidence or any other interlocutory ruling or order; and

(f) The relevant parts of any written exhibit (including affidavits) that present an issue on appeal.

30.1.6 Length. The optional contents of the record excerpts must not exceed 40 pages unless authorized by the court.

30.1.7 Form. The record excerpts must:

(a) Have a numbered table of contents, with citation to the record, beginning with the lower court docket sheet;

(b) Be on letter-size, light paper, reproduced by any process that results in a clear black image. Care must be taken to reproduce fully the document filing date column on the docket sheet;

(c) Be tabbed to correspond to the numbers assigned in the table of contents;

(d) Be bound to expose fully the filing date columns and allow the document to lie reasonably flat when opened. The record excerpts must have a durable white cover conforming to FED. R. APP. P. 32(a)(2), except that it will be denominated RECORD EXCERPTS.

The documents constituting the record excerpts do not need to be certified, but if the clerk's filed markings are either absent or not clearly legible, the accurate filing information must be typed or written thereon.

30.1.8 Nonconforming record excerpts. Record excerpts which do not conform to the requirements of this rule will be filed, but must be corrected within the time directed by the clerk. Failure to file corrected record excerpts may result in their being stricken and imposition of sanctions under 5TH CIR. R. 32.5.

30.2 Appendix - Agency Review Proceedings. *Petitions for review or enforcement of orders of an administrative agency, board, commission or officer must proceed on the original record on review, without a FED. R. APP. P. 30 required appendix. If a party requests use of the original record, the clerk may require payment of reasonable shipping costs, and the party is responsible for timely review and notification to the agency and the Fifth Circuit clerk's office of any record deficiencies, see 5TH CIR. R. 30.1.*

(a) If a certified list of documents comprising the record is filed in lieu of the formal record, petitioner must prepare and file with the court and serve on the agency, board, or commission a copy of the portions of the record relied upon by the parties in their briefs. The list of documents must be suitably covered, numbered, and indexed and filed within 21 days of the filing of respondent's brief.

(b) Except in review proceedings covered by 5TH CIR. R. 15.3, at the time of filing petitioner s brief, petitioner must file separately 4 copies of any order sought to be reviewed and any supporting opinion, findings of fact, or conclusions of law filed by the agency, board, commission, or officer.

FRAP 31. SERVING AND FILING BRIEFS

(a) *Time to Serve and File a Brief.*

(1) The appellant must serve and file a brief within 40 days after the record is filed. The appellee must serve and file a brief within 30 days after the appellant s brief is served. The appellant may serve and file a reply brief within 14 days after service of the appellee's brief but a reply brief must be filed at least 7 days before argument, unless the court, for good cause, allows a later filing.

(2) A court of appeals that routinely considers cases on the merits promptly after the briefs are filed may shorten the time to serve and file briefs, either by local rule or by order in a particular case.

(b) *Number of Copies.* Twenty-five copies of each brief must be filed with the clerk and 2 copies must be served on each unrepresented party and on counsel for each separately represented party. An unrepresented party proceeding in forma pauperis must file 4 legible copies with the clerk, and one copy must be served on each unrepresented party and on counsel for each separately represented party. The court may by local rule or by order in a particular case require the filing or service of a different number.

(c) *Consequence of Failure to File.* If an appellant fails to file a brief within the time provided by this rule, or within an extended time, an appellee may move to dismiss the appeal. An appellee who fails to file a brief will not be heard at oral argument unless the court grants permission.

FIFTH CIRCUIT RULE 31

31.1 Briefs - Number of Copies; Computer Generated Briefs. Only 7 paper copies of briefs need be filed. Where a party is represented by counsel who is exempt from electronic filing under 5TH CIR. R. 25.2, and counsel generates his or her brief by computer, the party also must submit an electronic version of the brief to the court. The filing party must serve unrepresented parties and counsel for separately represented parties in accordance with FED. R. APP. P. 31(b), and also must serve an electronic version of the brief on each party separately represented. However, the parties may agree in writing to waive service of paper copies of the brief and to be served with an electronic copy only. Electronic service may be in a form agreed to in writing by the parties, or by the same means as submitted to the court. The electronic copy of the brief must be filed on a CD, computer diskette, or such other electronic medium as the clerk may authorize.

The electronic version must:

be prepared in a single Portable Document Format (PDF) file. (Briefs scanned into PDF are not acceptable);

contain nothing other than the brief;

have as the first page of the electronic file a brief cover page as required by FED. R. APP. P. 32(a)(2).

If submitted on a CD, diskette, or other authorized physical media, the electronic version must have a label containing the case name and docket number, and identifying the brief as the appellant s, appellee s, etc.

The proof of service must comply with FED. R. APP. P. 25(d)(1)(B) & (2).

31.2   Briefs - Time for Filing Briefs of Intervenors or Amicus Curiae. *The time for filing the brief of the intervenor or amicus is extended until 7 days after the filing of the principal brief of the party supported by the intervenor or amicus.*

31.3   Briefs - Time for Mailing or Delivery to a Commercial Carrier. *The appellant must send his or her brief to the clerk not later than 40 days after the date of the briefing notice. Pursuant to FED. R. APP. P. 26(c), the appellee has 33 days from the appellant s date of the certificate of service to place the appellee s brief in the mail, file it with the clerk electronically where permitted, or to give it to a third-party commercial carrier for delivery within 3 days. This rule may not be combined with the additional time provisions of FED. R. APP. P. 26(c) to give the appellee 36 days to file a brief. The certificate of service required by FED. R. APP. P. 25(d) is placed in the brief as specified in 5TH CIR. R. 28.3, and must be dated. See 5TH CIR. R. 39.2 for limitations on recovery of certain mailing and commercial delivery costs.*

31.4   Briefs - Time for Filing.

31.4.1 General Provisions. The court expects briefs to be filed timely and without extensions in the vast majority of cases. No extensions are automatic, even where the request is unopposed. Any requests for extensions should be made sparingly. No extension can be granted without good cause shown as required by FED. R. APP. P. 26(b), or without meeting the additional requirements contained in the 5TH CIR. R.

(a) A request for extension should be made as soon as it is reasonably possible to foresee the need for the extension. The clerk must receive a request for extension at least 7 days before the due date, unless the movant demonstrates, in detail, that the facts that form

the basis of the motion either did not exist earlier or were not and with due diligence could not have been known earlier.

(b) *As specified in 5TH CIR. R. 27.1, the movant must indicate that all other parties have been contacted and whether the motion is opposed. Movants should request only as much time as is absolutely needed. The pendency of a motion for extension does not toll the time for compliance.*

31.4.2 *Grounds for Extensions. As justification for extensions, generalities, such as that the purpose of the motion is not for delay or that counsel is too busy, are not sufficient. Grounds that may merit consideration for extensions are, without limitation, the following, which must be set forth if claimed as a reason in any motion for an extension beyond 30 days:*

(a) *Engagement of counsel in other litigation, provided such litigation is identified by caption, number, and court, and there is set forth:*

(1) *A description of any effort taken to defer the other litigation and of any ruling thereon;*

(2) *An explanation of why other litigation should receive priority over the case at hand; and*

(3) *Other relevant circumstances, including why other associated counsel cannot prepare the brief or relieve the movant s counsel of the other litigation.*

(b) *The matter is so complex that an adequate brief cannot reasonably be prepared when due.*

(c) *Extreme hardship will result unless an extension is granted, in which event the nature of the hardship must be set forth in detail.*

31.4.3 *Levels of Extensions. There are two levels of extensions: a Level 1 extension of 1-30 days from the original due date; and a Level 2 extension of more than 30 days from the original due date.*

31.4.3.1 *Level 1 Extensions. The clerk is authorized to act on or refer to the court Level 1 extensions. The court prefers that an unopposed request be made by telephone, but it may be by written motion or letter. When making the request, the movant must explain what good cause exists for the extension. If the extension is granted by telephone, the movant will immediately send a confirming letter to the clerk, with copies to all parties.*

An opposed request for a Level 1 extension must be made by written motion setting forth why there is good cause. The motion must state the initial due date, whether any other extension has been granted, the length of the requested extension, and which parties have expressed opposition.

31.4.3.2 Level 2 Extensions. The clerk is authorized to act on or refer to the court Level 2 extensions. The request must be made by written motion, with copies to all parties, stating the initial due date, whether any other extension has been granted, the length of the requested extension, and whether the motion is opposed.

More than ordinary good cause is required for a Level 2 extension, and Level 2 extensions will be granted only under the most extraordinary of circumstances. The movant must demonstrate diligence and substantial need and must show in detail what special circumstances exist that make a Level 1 extension insufficient.

31.4.4 Extensions for Reply Briefs. The court greatly disfavors all extensions of time for filing reply briefs. The court assumes that the parties have had ample opportunity to present their arguments in their initial briefs and that extensions for reply briefs only delay submission of the case to the court.

I.O.P. - THE COURT CONTINUES TO RECEIVE A LARGE NUMBER OF MOTIONS REQUESTING EXTENSIONS OF TIME TO FILE BRIEFS, OR TO FILE BRIEFS OUT OF TIME, WHICH ARE CONSIDERED EXTENSION REQUESTS. THE MAJORITY OF THESE MOTIONS WERE BY COUNSEL, AND FREQUENTLY WERE MADE IN DIRECT CRIMINAL APPEALS WHICH HAVE THE LONGEST AVERAGE PROCESSING TIME FROM FILING THE NOTICE OF APPEAL TO FILING THE LAST BRIEF. TO ASSURE THAT THIS COURT DECIDES CASES MORE EXPEDITIOUSLY, THE COURT'S GOALS ARE TO: 1) REDUCE THE NUMBER OF MOTIONS TO EXTEND TIME TO FILE BRIEFS; AND 2) TO SHORTEN THE AMOUNT OF TIME GRANTED. IN GENERAL AND ABSENT THE MOST COMPELLING OF REASONS, NO MORE THAN 30 DAYS EXTENSION OF TIME WILL BE GRANTED IN CRIMINAL CASES AND NO MORE THAN 40 DAYS EXTENSION OF TIME WILL BE GRANTED IN CIVIL CASES.

FRAP 32. FORM OF BRIEFS, APPENDICES, AND OTHER PAPERS

(a) *Form of a Brief.*

(1) *Reproduction.*

(A) A brief may be reproduced by any process that yields a clear black image on light paper. The paper must be opaque and unglazed. Only one side of the paper may be used.

(B) Text must be reproduced with a clarity that equals or exceeds the output of a laser printer.

(C) Photographs, illustrations, and tables may be reproduced by any method that results in a good copy of the original; a glossy finish is acceptable if the original is glossy.

(2) *Cover.* Except for filings by unrepresented parties, the cover of the appellant's brief must be blue; the appellee s, red; an intervenor s or amicus curiae s, green; any reply brief, gray; and any supplemental brief, tan. The front cover of a brief must contain:

(A) the number of the case centered at the top;

(B) the name of the court;

(C) the title of the case (see Rule 12(a));

(D) the nature of the proceeding (e.g., Appeal, Petition for Review) and the name of the court, agency, or board below;

(E) the title of the brief, identifying the party or parties for whom the brief is filed; and

(F) the name, office address, and telephone number of counsel representing the party for whom the brief is filed.

(3) *Binding.* The brief must be bound in any manner that is secure, does not obscure the text, and permits the brief to lie reasonably flat when open.

(4) *Paper Size, Line Spacing, and Margins.* The brief must be on 8½ by 11 inch paper. The text must be double-spaced, but quotations more than two lines long may be indented and single-spaced. Headings and footnotes may be single-spaced. Margins must be at least one inch on all four sides. Page numbers may be placed in the margins, but no text may appear there.

(5) *Typeface.* Either a proportionally spaced or a monospaced face may be used.

　(A) A proportionally spaced face must include serifs, but sans-serif type may be used in headings and captions. A proportionally spaced face must be 14-point or larger.

　(B) A monospaced face may not contain more than 10½ characters per inch.

(6) *Type Styles.* A brief must be set in a plain, roman style, although italics or boldface may be used for emphasis. Case names must be italicized or underlined.

(7) *Length.*

　(A) *Page limitation.* A principal brief may not exceed 30 pages, or a reply brief 15 pages, unless it complies with Rule 32(a)(7)(B) and (C).

　(B) *Type-volume limitation.*

　　(i) A principal brief is acceptable if:

- it contains no more than 14,000 words; or
- it uses a monospaced face and contains no more than 1,300 lines of text.

　　(ii) A reply brief is acceptable if it contains no more than half of the type volume specified in Rule 32(a)(7)(B)(i).

　　(iii) Headings, footnotes, and quotations count toward the word and line limitations. The corporate disclosure statement, table of contents, table of citations, statement with respect to oral argument, any addendum containing statutes, rules or regulations, and any certificates of counsel do not count toward the limitation.

　(C) *Certificate of compliance.*

　　(i) A brief submitted under Rules 28.1(e)(2) or 32(a)(7)(B) must include a certificate by the attorney, or an unrepresented party, that the brief complies with the type-volume limitation. The person preparing the certificate may rely on the word or line count of the word-processing system used to prepare the brief. The certificate must state either:

- the number of words in the brief; or
- the number of lines of monospaced type in the brief.

(ii) Form 6 in the Appendix of Forms is a suggested form of a certificate of compliance. Use of Form 6 must be regarded as sufficient to meet the requirements of Rules 28.1(e)(3) and 32(a)(7)(C)(i).

(b) *Form of an Appendix.* An appendix must comply with Rule 32(a)(1), (2), (3), and (4), with the following exceptions:

(1) The cover of a separately bound appendix must be white.

(2) An appendix may include a legible photocopy of any document found in the record or of a printed judicial or agency decision.

(3) When necessary to facilitate inclusion of odd-sized documents such as technical drawings, an appendix may be a size other than 8½ by 11 inches, and need not lie reasonably flat when opened.

(c) *Form of Other Papers.*

(1) *Motion.* The form of a motion is governed by Rule 27(d).

(2) *Other Papers.* Any other paper, including a petition for panel rehearing and a petition for hearing or rehearing en banc, and any response to such a petition, must be reproduced in the manner prescribed by Rule 32(a), with the following exceptions:

(A) A cover is not necessary if the caption and signature page of the paper together contain the information required by Rule 32(a)(2). If a cover is used, it must be white.

(B) Rule 32(a)(7) does not apply.

(d) *Signature.* Every brief, motion, or other paper filed with the court must be signed by the party filing the paper or, if the party is represented, by one of the party s attorneys.

(e) *Local Variation.* Every court of appeals must accept documents that comply with the form requirements of this rule. By local rule or order in a particular case a court of appeals may accept documents that do not meet all of the form requirements of this rule.

FIFTH CIRCUIT RULE 32

32.1 Typeface. Must comply with FED. R. APP. P. 32(a)(5), except that footnotes may be 12 point or larger in proportionally spaced typeface, or 12½ characters per inch or larger in monospaced typeface.

32.2 Type Volume Limitations. *See* FED. R. APP. P. *32(a)(7)(B)(iii), and for cross-appeals,* FED. R. APP. P. *28.1(e). The certificate of interested parties does not count toward the limitation.*

32.3 Certificate of Compliance. *See Form 6 in the Appendix of Forms to the* FED. R. APP. P. *A material misrepresentation in the certificate of compliance may result in striking the brief and in sanctions against the person signing the brief.*

32.4 Motions for Extra-Length Briefs. *A motion to file a brief in excess of the page length or word-volume limitations must be filed at least 10 days in advance of the brief's due date. The court looks upon such motions with great disfavor and will grant them only for extraordinary and compelling reasons. If a motion to file an extra-length brief is submitted, a draft copy of the brief must be submitted with the motion.*

32.5 Rejection of Briefs and Record Excerpts. *If all copies of briefs and record excerpts do not conform to* 5TH CIR. R. *28 and 30 and all provisions of* FED. R. APP. P. *32, the clerk will file the briefs and record excerpts, but is authorized to return all nonconforming copies. An extension of 10 days is allowed for resubmission in a conforming format. The court may strike briefs and record excerpts if the party fails to submit conforming briefs or record excerpts within 14 days. If at any time the clerk believes the non-conformance is egregious or in bad faith, the clerk, in the alternative to filing the nonconforming matters, may submit them to a single judge, who can reject them and direct that they be returned unfiled. Failure to submit conforming briefs or record excerpts may result in imposition of sanctions.*

I.O.P. - FORM OF RECORD EXCERPTS/APPENDIX - SEE 5TH CIR. R. 30.

FRAP 32.1 CITING JUDICIAL DISPOSITIONS

(a) *Citation Permitted.* A court may not prohibit or restrict the citation of federal judicial opinions, orders, judgments, or other written dispositions that have been:

(1) designated as "unpublished," "not for publication," "non-precedential," "not precedent, or the like; and

(2) issued on or after January 1, 2007.

(b) *Copies Required.* If a party cites a federal judicial opinion, order, judgment, or other written disposition that is not available in a publicly accessible electronic database, the party must file and serve a copy of that opinion, order, judgment, or disposition with the brief or other paper in which it is cited.

FRAP 33. APPEAL CONFERENCES

The court may direct the attorneys and, when appropriate, the parties to participate in one or more conferences to address any matter that may aid in disposing of the proceedings, including simplifying the issues and discussing settlement. A judge or other person designated by the court may preside over the conference, which may be conducted in person or by telephone. Before a settlement conference, the attorneys must consult with their clients and obtain as much authority as feasible to settle the case. The court may, as a result of the conference, enter an order controlling the course of the proceedings or implementing any settlement agreement.

I.O.P. - APPEAL CONFERENCES - SEE 5TH CIR. R. 15.3.5.

FRAP 34. ORAL ARGUMENT

(a) *In General.*

    (1) *Party's Statement.* Any party may file, or a court may require by local rule, a statement explaining why oral argument should, or need not, be permitted.

    (2) *Standards.* Oral argument must be allowed in every case unless a panel of three judges who have examined the briefs and record unanimously agrees that oral argument is unnecessary for any of the following reasons:

        (A) the appeal is frivolous;

        (B) the dispositive issue or issues have been authoritatively decided; or

        (C) the facts and legal arguments are adequately presented in the briefs and record, and the decisional process would not be significantly aided by oral argument.

(b) *Notice of Argument; Postponement.* The clerk must advise all parties whether oral argument will be scheduled, and, if so, the date, time, and place for it, and the time allowed for each side. A motion to postpone the argument or to allow longer argument must be filed reasonably in advance of the hearing date.

(c) *Order and Contents of Argument.* The appellant opens and concludes the argument. Counsel must not read at length from briefs, records, or authorities.

(d) *Cross-Appeals and Separate Appeals.* If there is a cross-appeal, Rule 28.1(b) determines which party is the appellant and which is the appellee for purposes of oral argument. Unless the court directs otherwise, a cross-appeal or separate appeal must be argued when the initial appeal is argued. Separate parties should avoid duplicative argument.

(e) *Nonappearance of a Party.* If the appellee fails to appear for argument, the court must hear appellant's argument. If the appellant fails to appear for argument, the court may hear the appellee's argument. If neither party appears, the case will be decided on the briefs, unless the court orders otherwise.

(f) *Submission on Briefs.* The parties may agree to submit a case for decision on the briefs, but the court may direct that the case be argued.

(g) *Use of Physical Exhibits at Argument; Removal.* Counsel intending to use physical exhibits other than documents at the argument must arrange to place them in the courtroom on the day of the argument before the court convenes. After the argument, counsel must remove the exhibits from the courtroom, unless the court directs otherwise. The clerk may destroy or dispose of the exhibits if counsel does not reclaim them within a reasonable time after the clerk gives notice to remove them.

FIFTH CIRCUIT RULE 34

34.1 Docket Control. *In the interest of docket control, the chief judge may from time to time appoint a panel or panels to review pending cases for appropriate assignment or disposition under this rule or any other rule of this court.*

34.2 Oral Arguments. *Oral argument is governed by FED. R. APP. P. 34. Cases not set for oral argument are placed on the summary calendar for decision. The clerk will calendar the oral argument cases based upon the court's calendaring priorities. Counsel for each party must present oral argument unless excused by the court for good cause. The oral argument docket will show the time the court has allotted for each argument. If counsel for all parties indicate that oral argument is not necessary under paragraph .3 of this rule, the case will be governed by FED. R. APP. P. 34(f).*

34.3 Submission Without Argument. *A party desiring to waive oral argument in a case set for oral argument must file a motion to waive argument at least 7 days before the date set for hearing.*

34.4 Number of Counsel To Be Heard. *Not more than 2 counsel will be heard for each party on the argument of a case, and the time allowed may be apportioned between counsel in their discretion.*

34.5 Expediting Appeals. *The court may, on its own motion or for good cause on motion of either party, advance any case for hearing, and prescribe an abbreviated briefing schedule.*

34.6 Continuance of Hearing. *After a case has been set for hearing, the parties or counsel may not stipulate to delay the hearing. Only the court may delay argument for good cause shown. Engagement of counsel in other courts ordinarily is not considered good cause.*

34.7 Recording of Oral Arguments. *No cameras, tape recorders, or other equipment designed for the recording or transmission of visual images or sound may be present or used during oral argument. However, with the advance approval of the presiding judge, counsel may arrange, at their own expense, for a qualified court reporter to record and transcribe oral argument. If it is the court reporter's usual practice, the reporter may make and use a sound recording for the sole purpose of preparing an accurate transcript. The reporter may not make any recordings of the oral argument available to counsel, a party, or any other person until the court posts its recording of the oral argument on the court's Internet website.*

34.8 Criminal Justice Act Cases. The court expects court-appointed counsel to present oral argument. An associate attorney not appointed under the act may present argument only under the most pressing and unusual circumstances, and upon the court's advance authorization.

34.9 Checking In with Clerk's Office. On the day of hearing counsel must check in with the clerk 30 minutes before court convenes to confirm the name of the attorney or attorneys who will present argument for each party and how the argument time will be divided between opening and rebuttal. All counsel in the fourth and fifth cases on the docket heard in New Orleans may check in by telephone, but must report in person to the clerk's office within one hour after court convenes. On the last day of a New Orleans session, all attorneys must report in person to the clerk's office 30 minutes before court convenes.

34.10 Submission Without Argument. When a case is placed on the oral argument calendar, a judge of the court has determined that oral argument would be helpful. Therefore, requests of the parties to waive oral argument are not looked upon with favor, and counsel may be excused only by the court for good cause. See 5TH CIR. R. 34.3.

If appellant fails to appear in a criminal appeal from conviction, the court will not hear argument from the United States.

34.11 Time for Oral Argument. The time allowed for oral argument is indicated on the printed calendar. Most cases are allowed 20 minutes to the side. The word "side" refers to parties in their position on appeal. Where in doubt, consult the clerk's office.

34.12 Additional Time for Oral Argument. Additional time for oral argument is sparingly permitted. Requests for additional time should be set forth in a motion or letter to the clerk filed well in advance of the oral argument.

34.13 Calling the Calendar. The court usually does not call the calendar unless there are special problems requiring attention. The court hears the cases in the order they appear on the calendar.

I.O.P. - SCREENING - SCREENING IS THE NAME GIVEN TO THE METHOD USED BY THE COURT TO DETERMINE WHETHER CASES SHOULD BE ARGUED ORALLY OR DECIDED ON BRIEFS ONLY. THIS IS DONE UNDER FED. R. APP. P. AND 5TH CIR. R. 34.

(A) THE JUDGES OF THE COURT SCREEN CASES WITH ASSISTANCE FROM THE STAFF ATTORNEY. WHEN THE LAST BRIEF IS FILED, A CASE IS GENERALLY SENT TO THE STAFF ATTORNEY FOR PRESCREENING CLASSIFICATION. IF THE STAFF ATTORNEY CONCLUDES THAT THE CASE DOES NOT WARRANT ORAL ARGUMENT, A BRIEF MEMORANDUM MAY BE PREPARED AND THE CASE RETURNED TO THE CLERK. THE CLERK THEN ROUTES THE CASE TO 1 OF THE COURT'S JUDGES, SELECTED IN ROTATION. IF THAT JUDGE AGREES THAT THE CASE DOES NOT WARRANT ORAL ARGUMENT, THE

BRIEFS, TOGETHER WITH A PROPOSED OPINION, ARE FORWARDED TO THE 2 OTHER JUDGES ON THE SCREENING PANEL. IF ANY PARTY REQUESTS ORAL ARGUMENT, ALL PANEL JUDGES MUST CONCUR THAT THE CASE DOES NOT WARRANT ORAL ARGUMENT, AND ALSO IN THE PANEL OPINION AS A PROPER DISPOSITION WITHOUT ANY SPECIAL CONCURRENCE OR DISSENT. IF NO PARTY REQUESTS ORAL ARGUMENT, ALL PANEL JUDGES MUST CONCUR THAT THE CASE DOES NOT WARRANT ORAL ARGUMENT. HOWEVER, ABSENT A PARTY S REQUEST FOR ORAL ARGUMENT, SUMMARY DISPOSITION MAY INCLUDE A CONCURRENCE OR A DISSENT BY PANEL MEMBERS.

(B) IF THE STAFF ATTORNEY CONCLUDES THAT ORAL ARGUMENT IS REQUIRED, THE CASE IS SENT TO AN ACTIVE JUDGE FOR SCREENING. IF THE SCREENING JUDGE AGREES, THE CASE IS PLACED ON THE NEXT APPROPRIATE CALENDAR, CONSISTENT WITH THE COURT S CALENDARING PRIORITIES. IF THE SCREENING JUDGE DISAGREES WITH THE RECOMMENDATION FOR ORAL ARGUMENT, THAT JUDGE'S SCREENING PANEL DISPOSES OF THE CASE UNDER THE SUMMARY CALENDAR PROCEDURE.

DECISION WITHOUT ORAL ARGUMENT - WHEN ALL PANEL MEMBERS AGREE THAT ORAL ARGUMENT OF A CASE IS NOT NEEDED, THEY ADVISE THE CLERK THE CASE HAS BEEN PLACED ON THE SUMMARY CALENDAR. THE COURT'S DECISION USUALLY ACCOMPANIES THE NOTICE TO THE CLERK.

COURT YEAR SCHEDULE - THE CLERK PREPARES A PROPOSED COURT SCHEDULE FOR AN ENTIRE YEAR WHICH IS APPROVED BY THE SCHEDULING PROCTOR AND CHIEF JUDGE OF THE COURT. THE COURT SCHEDULE DOES NOT CONSIDER WHAT SPECIFIC CASES ARE TO BE HEARD, BUT ONLY SETS THE WEEKS OF COURT IN RELATION TO THE PROBABLE VOLUME OF CASES AND JUDGE POWER AVAILABILITY FOR THE YEAR.

JUDGE ASSIGNMENTS

PANEL SELECTION PROCEDURE - BASED ON THE NUMBER OF WEEKS EACH ACTIVE JUDGE SITS AND THE NUMBER OF SITTINGS AVAILABLE FROM THE COURT'S SENIOR JUDGES, AND VISITING CIRCUIT OR DISTRICT JUDGES, THE SCHEDULING PROCTOR AND CLERK CREATE PANELS OF JUDGES FOR THE SESSIONS OF THE COURT FOR THE ENTIRE COURT YEAR. THE JUDGES ARE SCHEDULED TO AVOID REPETITIVE SCHEDULING OF PANELS COMPOSED OF THE SAME MEMBERS.

SEPARATION OF ASSIGNMENT OF JUDGES AND CALENDARING OF CASES - THE JUDGE ASSIGNMENTS ARE MADE AVAILABLE ONLY TO THE JUDGES FOR THEIR ADVANCE PLANNING OF THEIR WORKLOAD FOR THE FORTHCOMING COURT YEAR. TO INSURE COMPLETE OBJECTIVITY IN THE ASSIGNMENT OF JUDGES AND THE CALENDARING OF CASES, THE TWO FUNCTIONS OF (1) JUDGE ASSIGNMENTS TO PANELS AND (2) CALENDARING OF CASES ARE CAREFULLY SEPARATED.

Preparation and Publishing Calendars

General - The clerk prepares calendars of cases under calendaring guidelines established by the court. Calendars are prepared for the number of sessions (usually between 3 and 5) scheduled for a month. Information about the names of the panel members is not disclosed within the clerk's office until the calendars of cases for the month are actually prepared so that briefs and other materials can be distributed.

Calendaring by Case Type - The clerk balances the calendars by dividing the cases evenly among the panels by case type so that each panel for a particular month has more or less an equal number of different types of litigation for consideration.

Preference Cases - The categories of cases listed in 5th Cir. R. 47.7 are given preference in processing and disposition. To assist the clerk in implementing this rule, any party to a civil appeal or review proceeding requiring priority status should notify the clerk and cite the statutory support for the preference.

Non-Preference Cases - All other cases are calendared for hearing in accordance with the court's "first-in first-out" rule. Unless the court assigns special priority the oldest cases in point of time of availability of briefs are ordinarily calendared first for hearing.

Calendaring for Convenience of Counsel - For the New Orleans sessions, cases with non-local lawyers are scheduled in the first positions on the calendar whenever possible for their convenience in making departure accommodations.

Number of Cases Assigned - Unless special provision is made, a regular session of a panel of the court will hear 5 cases per day for 4 days, Monday through Thursday.

Advance Notice - The court seeks to give counsel 60 days advance notice of cases set for oral argument.

Forwarding Briefs to Judges - Immediately after formally issuing the calendar the clerk sends the panel members copies of the briefs for the cases set on the calendar.

Pre-Argument Preparation - The judges invariably read all briefs prior to oral argument.

IDENTITY OF PANEL - The clerk may not disclose the names of the panel members for a particular session until 1 week in advance of the session.

ORAL ARGUMENT

PRESENTING ARGUMENT - Counsel should prepare their oral arguments knowing the judges have already studied the briefs. Reading from briefs, decisions, or the record is not permitted except in unusual circumstances. Counsel should be prepared to answer the court's questions. The court will consider a motion to extend the time allotted for argument if the court's questions prevent completion of counsel's argument.

LIGHTING SIGNAL PROCEDURE - The courtroom deputy will keep track of the time using lighting signals:

(A) **APPELLANT'S ARGUMENT** - A green light signals the beginning of the opening argument of appellant. Two minutes before expiration of the time allowed for opening argument, the green light goes off and a yellow light comes on. When the time reserved for opening argument expires, the yellow light goes off and a red light comes on. If counsel proceeds after the red light, time will be deducted from the rebuttal period.

(B) **APPELLEE'S ARGUMENT** - The same procedure as outlined above is used.

(C) **APPELLANT'S REBUTTAL** - A green light signals commencement of time; a red light comes on when time expires. No yellow light is used.

CASE CONFERENCES AND DESIGNATION OF WRITING JUDGE - The panel hearing the arguments usually confers on the cases at the conclusion of each day's arguments. A tentative decision is reached and the presiding judge assigns responsibility for opinion writing. There is no pre-argument assignment of opinion writing. Judges do not specialize. Assignments are made to equalize the workload of the entire session.

FRAP 35. EN BANC DETERMINATION

(a) *When Hearing or Rehearing En Banc May Be Ordered.* A majority of the circuit judges who are in regular active service and who are not disqualified may order that an appeal or other proceeding be heard or reheard by the court of appeals en banc. An en banc hearing or rehearing is not favored and ordinarily will not be ordered unless:

(1) en banc consideration is necessary to secure or maintain uniformity of the court's decisions; or

(2) the proceeding involves a question of exceptional importance.

(b) *Petition for Hearing or Rehearing En Banc.* A party may petition for a hearing or rehearing en banc.

(1) The petition must begin with a statement that either:

(A) the panel decision conflicts with a decision of the United States Supreme Court or of the court to which the petition is addressed (with citation to the conflicting case or cases) and consideration by the full court is therefore necessary to secure and maintain uniformity of the court's decisions; or

(B) the proceeding involves one or more questions of exceptional importance, each of which must be concisely stated; for example, a petition may assert that a proceeding presents a question of exceptional importance if it involves an issue on which the panel decision conflicts with the authoritative decisions of other United States Courts of Appeals that have addressed the issue.

(2) Except by the court's permission, a petition for an en banc hearing or rehearing must not exceed 15 pages, excluding material not counted under Rule 32.

(3) For purposes of the page limit in Rule 35(b)(2), if a party files both a petition for panel rehearing and a petition for rehearing en banc, they are considered a single document even if they are filed separately, unless separate filing is required by local rule.

(c) *Time for Petition for Hearing or Rehearing En Banc.* A petition that an appeal be heard initially en banc must be filed by the date when the appellee's brief is due. A petition for a rehearing en banc must be filed within the time prescribed by Rule 40 for filing a petition for rehearing.

(d) *Number of Copies.* The number of copies to be filed must be prescribed by local rule and may be altered by order in a particular case.

(e) *Response.* No response may be filed to a petition for an en banc consideration unless the court orders a response.

(f) *Call for a Vote.* A vote need not be taken to determine whether the case will be heard or reheard en banc unless a judge calls for a vote.

FIFTH CIRCUIT RULE 35

35.1 Caution. *Counsel are reminded that in every case the duty of counsel is fully discharged without filing a petition for rehearing en banc unless the case meets the rigid standards of FED. R. APP. P. 35(a). As is noted in FED. R. APP. P. 35, en banc hearing or rehearing is not favored. Among the reasons is that each request for en banc consideration must be studied by every active judge of the court and is a serious call on limited judicial resources. Counsel have a duty to the court commensurate with that owed their clients to read with attention and observe with restraint the standards of FED. R. APP. P. 35(b)(1). The court takes the view that, given the extraordinary nature of petitions for en banc consideration, it is fully justified in imposing sanctions on its own initiative under, inter alia, FED. R. APP. P. 38 and 28 U.S.C. § 1927, upon the person who signed the petitions, the represented party, or both, for manifest abuse of the procedure.*

35.2 Form of Petition. *Twenty copies of every petition for en banc consideration, whether upon initial hearing or rehearing, must be filed. The petition must not be incorporated in the petition for rehearing before the panel, if one is filed, but must be complete in itself. In no case will a petition for en banc consideration adopt by reference any matter from the petition for panel rehearing or from any other briefs or motions in the case. A petition for en banc consideration must contain the following items, in order:*

35.2.1 Certificate of interested persons required for briefs by 5TH CIR. R. 28.2.1.

35.2.2 If the party petitioning for en banc consideration is represented by counsel, a statement as set forth in FED. R. APP. P. 35(b)(1).

35.2.3 Table of contents and authorities.

35.2.4 Statement of the issue or issues asserted to merit en banc consideration. It will rarely occur that these will be the same as those appropriate for panel rehearing. A petition for en banc consideration must be limited to the circumstances enumerated in FED. R. APP. P. 35(a).

35.2.5 Statement of the course of proceedings and disposition of the case.

35.2.6 Statement of any facts necessary to the argument of the issues.

35.2.7 Argument and authorities. These will concern only the issues required by paragraph (.2.4) hereof and shall address specifically, not only their merit, but why they are contended to be worthy of en banc consideration.

35.2.8 Conclusion.

35.2.9 Certificate of service.

35.2.10 A copy of the opinion or order sought to be reviewed. The opinion or order will be bound with the petition and shall not be marked or annotated.

35.3 Response to Petition. No response to a petition for en banc consideration will be received unless requested by the court.

35.4 Time and Form - Extensions. Any petition for rehearing en banc must be received in the clerk's office within the time specified in FED. R. APP. P. 40. Counsel should not request extensions of time except for the most compelling reasons.

35.5 Length. See FED. R. APP. P. 35(b)(2).

35.6 Determination of Causes En Banc and Composition of En Banc Court. A cause will be heard or reheard en banc when it meets the criteria for en banc set out in FED. R. APP. P. 35(a).

The en banc court will be composed of all active judges of the court plus any senior judge of the court who participated in the panel decision who elects to participate in the en banc consideration. This election is to be communicated timely to the chief judge and clerk. Any judge participating in an en banc poll, hearing, or rehearing while in regular active service who subsequently takes senior status may elect to continue participating in the final resolution of the case.

I.O.P.

PETITION FOR REHEARING EN BANC

EXTRAORDINARY NATURE OF PETITIONS FOR REHEARING EN BANC - A PETITION FOR REHEARING EN BANC IS AN EXTRAORDINARY PROCEDURE THAT IS INTENDED TO BRING TO THE ATTENTION OF THE ENTIRE COURT AN ERROR OF EXCEPTIONAL PUBLIC IMPORTANCE OR AN OPINION THAT DIRECTLY CONFLICTS WITH PRIOR SUPREME COURT, FIFTH CIRCUIT OR STATE LAW PRECEDENT, SUBJECT TO THE FOLLOWING: ALLEGED ERRORS IN THE FACTS OF THE CASE (INCLUDING SUFFICIENCY OF THE EVIDENCE) OR IN THE APPLICATION OF CORRECT PRECEDENT TO THE FACTS OF THE CASE ARE GENERALLY MATTERS FOR PANEL REHEARING BUT NOT FOR REHEARING EN BANC.

THE MOST ABUSED PREROGATIVE - Petitions for rehearing en banc are the most abused prerogative of appellate advocates in the Fifth Circuit. Fewer than 1% of the cases decided by the court on the merits are reheard en banc; and frequently those rehearings granted result from a request for en banc reconsideration by a judge of the court rather than a petition by the parties.

Handling of Petition by the Judges

PANEL HAS CONTROL - Although each panel judge and every active judge receives a copy of the petition for rehearing en banc, the filing of a petition for rehearing en banc does not take the case out of the control of the panel deciding the case. A petition for rehearing en banc is treated as a petition for rehearing by the panel if no petition is filed. The panel may grant rehearing without action by the full court.

REQUESTING A POLL - Within 10 days of the filing of the petition, any active judge of the court or any member of the panel rendering the decision, who desires that the case be reheard en banc, may notify the writing judge (the senior active Fifth Circuit judge if the writing judge is a non-active member) to this effect on or before the date shown on the clerk's form that transmits the petition. This notification is also notice that if the panel declines to grant rehearing, an en banc poll is desired.

If the panel decides not to grant the rehearing after such notice, it notifies the chief judge, who then polls the court by written ballot on whether en banc rehearing should be granted.

REQUESTING A POLL ON COURT'S OWN MOTION - Any active member of the court or any member of the panel rendering the decision may request a poll of the active members of the court whether rehearing en banc should be granted, whether or not a party filed a petition for rehearing en banc. A requesting judge ordinarily sends a letter to the chief judge with copies to the other active judges of the court and any other panel member.

POLLING THE COURT - When a request to poll the court is made, each active judge of the court casts a ballot and sends a copy to all other active judges of the court and any senior Fifth Circuit judge who is a panel member. The ballot indicates whether the judge voting desires oral argument if en banc is granted.

NEGATIVE POLL - If the vote is unfavorable to the grant of en banc consideration, the chief judge advises the writing judge. The panel originally hearing the case then enters an appropriate order.

AFFIRMATIVE POLL - If a majority of the judges in active service who are not disqualified, vote for en banc hearing or rehearing, the Chief Judge instructs the Clerk as to an appropriate order. The order indicates a rehearing en banc with or without oral argument has been granted, and specifies a briefing schedule for filing of en banc briefs. The appellant's en banc brief will have a blue cover; the appellee's en banc brief will have a red cover.

Every party must then furnish to the Clerk 20 additional copies of every brief the party previously filed.

NO POLL REQUEST - If the specified time for requesting a poll has expired and the writing judge of the panel has not received a request from any active member of the court, or other panel member, the judge may take such action deemed appropriate on the petition. However, in the order disposing of the case and the petition, the panel s order denying the petition for rehearing en banc must show no poll was requested.

CAPITAL CASES - Consistent with long established legal principle and uniformly followed practice, the filing of a petition for rehearing (or hearing) en banc does not constitute or operate as a stay of execution and does not preclude carrying out an execution.

Timely petitions for rehearing (or hearing) en banc which are filed in a capital case while a scheduled execution date is pending and less than 22 days before the scheduled date will be processed and distributed in the manner prescribed by the Chief Judge or delegee. The Chief Judge or delegee may order expedited consideration thereof and set a time limit for each judge eligible to vote thereon to advise the Chief Judge or delegee whether to call for a poll and whether (if a poll is or were to be timely requested by any judge) the judge would vote for or against rehearing (or hearing) en banc, and the petition for rehearing (or hearing) en banc will be disposed of accordingly. If no poll is timely requested, or if a poll results in no rehearing (or hearing) en banc, the panel may enter an order denying rehearing (or hearing) en banc. If a poll results in a grant of rehearing (or hearing) en banc, the Chief Judge, or delegee, will enter an order staying the execution pending further order of the court.

FRAP 36. ENTRY OF JUDGMENT; NOTICE

(a) *Entry.* A judgment is entered when it is noted on the docket. The clerk must prepare, sign, and enter the judgment:

    (1) after receiving the court's opinion — but if settlement of the judgment's form is required, after final settlement; or

    (2) if a judgment is rendered without an opinion, as the court instructs.

(b) *Notice.* On the date when judgment is entered, the clerk must serve on all parties a copy of the opinion — or the judgment, if no opinion was written — and a notice of the date when the judgment was entered.

FRAP 37. INTEREST ON JUDGMENT

(a) *When the Court Affirms.* Unless the law provides otherwise, if a money judgment in a civil case is affirmed, whatever interest is allowed by law is payable from the date when the district court s judgment was entered.

(b) *When the Court Reverses.* If the court modifies or reverses a judgment with a direction that a money judgment be entered in the district court, the mandate must contain instructions about the allowance of interest.

FRAP 38. FRIVOLOUS APPEAL — DAMAGES AND COSTS

If a court of appeals determines that an appeal is frivolous, it may, after a separately filed motion or notice from the court and reasonable opportunity to respond, award just damages and single or double costs to the appellee.

FRAP 39. COSTS

(a) *Against Whom Assessed.* The following rules apply unless the law provides or the court orders otherwise:

  (1) if an appeal is dismissed, costs are taxed against the appellant, unless the parties agree otherwise;

  (2) if a judgment is affirmed, costs are taxed against the appellant;

  (3) if a judgment is reversed, costs are taxed against the appellee;

  (4) if a judgment is affirmed in part, reversed in part, modified, or vacated, costs are taxed only as the court orders.

(b) *Costs For and Against the United States.* Costs for or against the United States, its agency, or officer will be assessed under Rule 39(a) only if authorized by law.

(c) *Costs of Copies.* Each court of appeals must, by local rule, fix the maximum rate for taxing the cost of producing necessary copies of a brief or appendix, or copies of records authorized by Rule 30(f). The rate must not exceed that generally charged for such work in the area where the clerk's office is located and should encourage economical methods of copying.

(d) *Bill of Costs: Objections; Insertion in Mandate.*

  (1) A party who wants costs taxed must within 14 days after entry of judgment file with the circuit clerk, with proof of service, an itemized and verified bill of costs.

  (2) Objections must be filed within 14 days after service of the bill of costs, unless the court extends the time.

  (3) The clerk must prepare and certify an itemized statement of costs for insertion in the mandate, but issuance of the mandate must not be delayed for taxing costs. If the mandate issues before costs are finally determined, the district clerk must upon the circuit clerk's request add the statement of costs, or any amendment of it, to the mandate.

(e) *Costs on Appeal Taxable in the District Court.* The following costs on appeal are taxable in the district court for the benefit of the party entitled to costs under this rule:

  (1) the preparation and transmission of the record;

(2) the reporter's transcript, if needed to determine the appeal;

(3) premiums paid for a supersedeas bond or other bond to preserve rights pending appeal; and

(4) the fee for filing the notice of appeal.

FIFTH CIRCUIT RULE 39

39.1 Taxable Rates. The cost of reproducing necessary copies of the briefs, appendices, or record excerpts shall be taxed at a rate of actual cost, or $.15 per page, whichever is less, including cover, index, and internal pages, for any form of reproduction costs. The cost of the binding required by 5TH CIR. R. 32.2.3 that mandates that briefs must lie reasonably flat when open shall be a taxable cost but not limited to the foregoing rate. This rate is intended to approximate the current cost of the most economical acceptable method of reproduction generally available; and the clerk will, at reasonable intervals, examine and review it to reflect current rates. Taxable costs will be authorized for up to 15 copies for a brief and 10 copies of an appendix or record excerpts, unless the clerk gives advance approval for additional copies.

39.2 Nonrecovery of Mailing and Commercial Delivery Service Costs. Mailing and commercial delivery fees incurred in transmitting briefs are not recoverable as taxable costs.

39.3 Time for Filing Bills of Costs. The clerk must receive bills of costs and any objections within the times set forth in FED. R. APP. P. 39(d). See 5TH CIR. R. 26.1.

FRAP 40. PETITION FOR PANEL REHEARING

(a) *Time to File; Contents; Answer; Action by the Court if Granted.*

    (1) *Time.* Unless the time is shortened or extended by order or local rule, a petition for panel rehearing may be filed within 14 days after entry of judgment. But in a civil case, unless an order shortens or extends the time, the petition may be filed by any party within 45 days after entry of judgment if one of the parties is:

        (A) the United States;

        (B) a United States agency;

        (C) a United States officer or employee sued in an official capacity; or

        (D) a current or former United States officer or employee sued in an individual capacity for an act or omission occurring in connection with duties performed on the United States' behalf including all instances in which the United States represents that person when the court of appeals' judgment is entered or files the petition for that person.

    (2) *Contents.* The petition must state with particularity each point of law or fact that the petitioner believes the court has overlooked or misapprehended and must argue in support of the petition. Oral argument is not permitted.

    (3) *Answer.* Unless the court requests, no answer to a petition for panel rehearing is permitted. But ordinarily rehearing will not be granted in the absence of such a request.

    (4) *Action by the Court.* If a petition for panel rehearing is granted, the court may do any of the following:

        (A) make a final disposition of the case without reargument;

        (B) restore the case to the calendar for reargument or resubmission; or

        (C) issue any other appropriate order.

(b) *Form of Petition; Length.* The petition must comply in form with Rule 32. Copies must be served and filed as Rule 31 prescribes. Unless the court permits or a local rule provides otherwise, a petition for panel rehearing must not exceed 15 pages.

FIFTH CIRCUIT RULE 40

***40.1 Copies.** Four copies of all petitions for rehearing will be filed. A party seeking panel rehearing must attach to the petition an unmarked copy of the opinion or order sought to be reviewed. If the party contemporaneously files a petition for rehearing en banc and attaches a copy of the opinion or order required by 5TH CIR. R. 35.2.10, the party does not have to attach a copy to the petition for panel rehearing.*

***40.2 Limited Nature of Petition for Panel Rehearing.** A petition for rehearing is intended to bring to the attention of the panel claimed errors of fact or law in the opinion. It is not used for reargument of the issue previously presented or to attack the court's well-settled summary calendar procedures. Petitions for rehearing of panel decisions are reviewed by panel members only.*

***40.3 Length.** See FED. R. APP. P. 40(b).*

***40.4 Time for Filing.** The clerk must receive a petition for rehearing within the time prescribed in FED. R. APP. P. 40(a).*

I.O.P. - NECESSITY FOR FILING - IT IS NOT NECESSARY TO FILE A PETITION FOR REHEARING IN THE COURT OF APPEALS AS A PREREQUISITE TO FILING A PETITION FOR CERTIORARI IN THE SUPREME COURT OF THE UNITED STATES.

CAPITAL CASES - CONSISTENT WITH LONG ESTABLISHED LEGAL PRINCIPLE AND UNIFORMLY FOLLOWED PRACTICE, THE FILING OF A PETITION FOR REHEARING DOES NOT CONSTITUTE OR OPERATE AS A STAY OF EXECUTION AND DOES NOT PRECLUDE CARRYING OUT AN EXECUTION.

FRAP 41. MANDATE: CONTENTS; ISSUANCE AND EFFECTIVE DATE; STAY

(a) *Contents.* Unless the court directs that a formal mandate issue, the mandate consists of a certified copy of the judgment, a copy of the court's opinion, if any, and any direction about costs.

(b) *When Issued.* The court's mandate must issue 7 days after the time to file a petition for rehearing expires, or 7 days after entry of an order denying a timely petition for panel rehearing, petition for rehearing en banc, or motion for stay of mandate, whichever is later. The court may shorten or extend the time.

(c) *Effective Date.* The mandate is effective when issued.

(d) *Staying the Mandate.*

  (1) *On Petition for Rehearing or Motion.* The timely filing of a petition for panel rehearing, petition for rehearing en banc, or motion for stay of mandate, stays the mandate until disposition of the petition or motion, unless the court orders otherwise.

  (2) *Pending Petition for Certiorari.*

   (A) A party may move to stay the mandate pending the filing of a petition for a writ of certiorari in the Supreme Court. The motion must be served on all parties and must show that the certiorari petition would present a substantial question and that there is good cause for a stay.

   (B) The stay must not exceed 90 days, unless the period is extended for good cause or unless the party who obtained the stay files a petition for the writ and so notifies the circuit clerk in writing within the period of the stay. In that case, the stay continues until the Supreme Court's final disposition.

   (C) The court may require a bond or other security as a condition to granting or continuing a stay of the mandate.

   (D) The court of appeals must issue the mandate immediately when a copy of a Supreme Court order denying the petition for writ of certiorari is filed.

FIFTH CIRCUIT RULE 41

41.1 Stay of Mandate - Criminal Appeals. *A motion for a stay of the issuance of a mandate in a direct criminal appeal filed under* FED. R. APP. P. *41 will not be granted simply upon request. Unless the petition sets forth good cause for stay or clearly demonstrates that a substantial question is to be presented to the Supreme Court, the motion shall be denied and the mandate thereafter issued forthwith.*

41.2 Recall of Mandate. *Once issued a mandate will not be recalled except to prevent injustice.*

41.3 Effect of Granting Rehearing En Banc. *Unless otherwise expressly provided, the granting of a rehearing en banc vacates the panel opinion and judgment of the court and stays the mandate. If, after voting a case en banc, the court lacks a quorum to act on the case for 30 consecutive days, the case is automatically returned to the panel, the panel opinion is reinstated as an unpublished (and hence nonprecedential) opinion, and the mandate is released. To act on a case, the en banc court must have a quorum consisting of a majority of the en banc court as defined in 28 U.S.C. § 46(c).*

41.4 Issuance of Mandate in Expedited Appeals or Mandamus Actions. *The clerk will issue the mandate forthwith in any expedited appeal of a criminal sentence and in actions denying mandamus relief, unless instructed otherwise by the court.*

I.O.P. - ABSENT A MOTION FOR STAY OR A STAY BY OPERATION OF AN ORDER, RULE, OR PROCEDURE, MANDATES WILL ISSUE PROMPTLY ON THE 8TH DAY AFTER THE TIME FOR FILING A PETITION FOR REHEARING EXPIRES; OR AFTER ENTRY OF AN ORDER DENYING THE PETITION. AS AN EXCEPTION, AND BY COURT DIRECTION, THE CLERK WILL IMMEDIATELY ISSUE THE MANDATE WHEN THE COURT DISMISSES A CASE FOR FAILURE TO PROSECUTE AN APPEAL OR FOR LACK OF JURISDICTION, OR IN SUCH OTHER INSTANCES AS THE COURT MAY DIRECT. THE ORIGINAL RECORD AND ANY EXHIBITS WILL BE RETURNED TO THE CLERK OF THE DISTRICT COURT WITH THE MANDATE.

FED. R. APP. P. WITH 5TH CIR. R. & IOPs

FRAP 42. VOLUNTARY DISMISSAL

(a) *Dismissal in the District Court.* Before an appeal has been docketed by the circuit clerk, the district court may dismiss the appeal on the filing of a stipulation signed by all parties or on the appellant s motion with notice to all parties.

(b) *Dismissal in the Court of Appeals.* The circuit clerk may dismiss a docketed appeal if the parties file a signed dismissal agreement specifying how costs are to be paid and pay any fees that are due. But no mandate or other process may issue without a court order. An appeal may be dismissed on the appellant's motion on terms agreed to by the parties or fixed by the court.

FIFTH CIRCUIT RULE 42

42.1 Dismissal by Appellant. In all cases where the appellant or petitioner files an unopposed motion to withdraw the appeal or agency review proceeding, the clerk will enter an order of dismissal and issue a copy of the order as the mandate.

42.2 Frivolous and Unmeritorious Appeals. If upon the hearing of any interlocutory motion or as a result of a review under 5TH CIR. R. 34, it appears to the court that the appeal is frivolous and entirely without merit, the appeal will be dismissed.

42.3 Dismissal for Failure To Prosecute.

42.3.1 In direct criminal appeals proceeding in forma pauperis, the provisions of 5TH CIR. R. 42.3.1.1 and 42.3.1.2 apply. In habeas cases, actions filed under 28 U.S.C. § 2255, and other prisoner matters proceeding in forma pauperis, the provisions of 5TH CIR. R. 42.3.1.1 apply if the appellant is represented by counsel; prisoners proceeding pro se will be given an initial written deadline for filing a certificate of appealability, filing any briefs, for paying fees, or for complying with other directives of the court. If pro se prisoners do not meet the deadline established, or timely request an extension of time, the clerk will dismiss the appeal without further notice, 15 days after the deadline date.

42.3.1.1 Appeals with Counsel. If appellant is represented by appointed or retained counsel, the clerk will issue a notice to counsel that, upon expiration of 15 days from the date of the notice, the appeal may be dismissed for want of prosecution unless prior to that date the default is remedied, and must enter an order directing counsel to show cause within 15 days from the date of the order why disciplinary action should not be taken against counsel. If the default is remedied within that time, the clerk must not dismiss the appeal and may refer to the court the matter of disciplinary action against the attorney. If the default is not remedied within that time, the clerk may enter an order dismissing the appeal for want of prosecution or may refer to the court the question of dismissal. The clerk must refer to the court the matter of disciplinary action against the attorney. The court may refer the matter of disciplinary action to a special master including but not limited to a district or magistrate judge.

42.3.1.2 Appeals without Counsel. The clerk must issue a notice to appellant that 15 days from the date of the notice the appeal will be dismissed for want of prosecution, unless the default is remedied before that date. If the default is remedied within that time, the clerk must not dismiss the appeal.

42.3.2 In all other appeals when appellant fails to order the transcript, fails to file a brief, or otherwise fails to comply with the rules of the court, the clerk must dismiss the appeal for want of prosecution.

42.3.3 In all instances of failure to prosecute an appeal to hearing as required, the court may take such other action as it deems appropriate.

42.3.4 An order dismissing an appeal for want of prosecution must be issued to the clerk of the district court as the mandate.

***42.4 Dismissals Without Prejudice.** In acting on a motion under 5TH CIR. R. 27.1.3 to stay further proceedings, the clerk may enter such appeals or agency review proceedings as dismissed without prejudice to the right of reinstatement of the appeal within 180 days from the date of dismissal. Any party desiring reinstatement, or an extension of the time to seek reinstatement, must notify the clerk in writing within the time period allowed for reinstatement. This procedure does not apply where the stay is sought pending a decision of this court in another case, a decision of the Supreme Court, or a stay on the court's own motion. If the appeal is not reinstated within the period fixed, the appeal is deemed dismissed with prejudice. However, an additional period of 180 days from the date of dismissal will be allowed for applying for relief from a dismissal with prejudice which resulted from mistake, inadvertence, or excusable neglect of counsel or a pro se litigant.*

FRAP 43. SUBSTITUTION OF PARTIES

(a) *Death of a Party.*

(1) *After Notice of Appeal Is Filed.* If a party dies after a notice of appeal has been filed or while a proceeding is pending in the court of appeals, the decedent s personal representative may be substituted as a party on motion filed with the circuit clerk by the representative or by any party. A party's motion must be served on the representative in accordance with Rule 25. If the decedent has no representative, any party may suggest the death on the record, and the court of appeals may then direct appropriate proceedings.

(2) *Before Notice of Appeal Is Filed — Potential Appellant.* If a party entitled to appeal dies before filing a notice of appeal, the decedent s personal representative or, if there is no personal representative, the decedent's attorney of record may file a notice of appeal within the time prescribed by these rules. After the notice of appeal is filed, substitution must be in accordance with Rule 43(a)(1).

(3) *Before Notice of Appeal Is Filed — Potential Appellee.* If a party against whom an appeal may be taken dies after entry of a judgment or order in the district court, but before a notice of appeal is filed, an appellant may proceed as if the death had not occurred. After the notice of appeal is filed, substitution must be in accordance with Rule 43(a)(1).

(b) *Substitution for a Reason Other Than Death.* If a party needs to be substituted for any reason other than death, the procedure prescribed in Rule 43(a) applies.

(c) *Public Officer: Identification; Substitution.*

(1) *Identification of Party.* A public officer who is a party to an appeal or other proceeding in an official capacity may be described as a party by the public officer's official title rather than by name. But the court may require the public officer s name to be added.

(2) *Automatic Substitution of Officeholder.* When a public officer who is a party to an appeal or other proceeding in an official capacity dies, resigns, or otherwise ceases to hold office, the action does not abate. The public officer s successor is automatically substituted as a party. Proceedings following the substitution are to be in the name of the substituted party, but any misnomer that does not affect the substantial rights of the parties may be disregarded. An order of substitution may be entered at any time, but failure to enter an order does not affect the substitution.

FRAP 44. CASE INVOLVING A CONSTITUTIONAL QUESTION WHEN THE UNITED STATES OR THE RELEVANT STATE IS NOT A PARTY

(a) *Constitutional Challenge to Federal Statute.* If a party questions the constitutionality of an Act of Congress in a proceeding in which the United States or its agency, officer, or employee is not a party in an official capacity, the questioning party must give written notice to the circuit clerk immediately upon the filing of the record or as soon as the question is raised in the court of appeals. The clerk must then certify that fact to the Attorney General.

(b) *Constitutional Challenge to State Statute.* If a party questions the constitutionality of a statute of a State in a proceeding in which that State or its agency, officer, or employee is not a party in an official capacity, the questioning party must give written notice to the circuit clerk immediately upon the filing of the record or as soon as the question is raised in the court of appeals. The clerk must then certify that fact to the attorney general of the State.

FRAP 45. CLERK'S DUTIES

(a) *General Provisions.*

(1) *Qualifications.* The circuit clerk must take the oath and post any bond required by law. Neither the clerk nor any deputy clerk may practice as an attorney or counselor in any court while in office.

(2) *When Court Is Open.* The court of appeals is always open for filing any paper, issuing and returning process, making a motion, and entering an order. The clerk's office with the clerk or a deputy in attendance must be open during business hours on all days except Saturdays, Sundays, and legal holidays. A court may provide by local rule or by order that the clerk's office be open for specified hours on Saturdays or on legal holidays other than New Year s Day, Martin Luther King, Jr. s Birthday, Washington s Birthday, Memorial Day, Independence Day, Labor Day, Columbus Day, Veterans' Day, Thanksgiving Day, and Christmas Day.

(b) *Records.*

(1) *The Docket.* The circuit clerk must maintain a docket and an index of all docketed cases in the manner prescribed by the Director of the Administrative Office of the United States Courts. The clerk must record all papers filed with the clerk and all process, orders, and judgments.

(2) *Calendar.* Under the court s direction, the clerk must prepare a calendar of cases awaiting argument. In placing cases on the calendar for argument, the clerk must give preference to appeals in criminal cases and to other proceedings and appeals entitled to preference by law.

(3) *Other Records.* The clerk must keep other books and records required by the Director of the Administrative Office of the United States Courts, with the approval of the Judicial Conference of the United States, or by the court.

(c) *Notice of an Order or Judgment.* Upon the entry of an order or judgment, the circuit clerk must immediately serve a notice of entry on each party, with a copy of any opinion, and must note the date of service on the docket. Service on a party represented by counsel must be made on counsel.

(d) *Custody of Records and Papers.* The circuit clerk has custody of the court s records and papers. Unless the court orders or instructs otherwise, the clerk must not permit an original record or paper to be taken from the clerk's office. Upon disposition of the case, original papers constituting the record on appeal or review must be returned to the court or agency from which they were received. The clerk must preserve a copy of any brief, appendix, or other paper that has been filed.

FIFTH CIRCUIT RULE 45

45.1 Location. The clerk's office is maintained in the city of New Orleans, Louisiana.

45.2 Release of Original Papers. The clerk may release original records or papers without a court order for a limited time upon a party's or counsel's request, to facilitate preparation of a brief in a pending appeal.

45.3 Office To Be Open. The clerk's office is open for business on all days except Saturdays, Sundays, designated federal holidays, and Mardi Gras.

I.O.P. - OFFICE HOURS ARE FROM 8:00 A.M. TO 5:00 P.M. CENTRAL TIME MONDAY THROUGH FRIDAY.

(A) THE CLERK'S OFFICE WELCOMES TELEPHONE INQUIRIES FROM COUNSEL CONCERNING RULES AND PROCEDURES. TELEPHONE NO. (504) 310-7700.

(B) IN EMERGENCY SITUATIONS AFTER NORMAL OFFICE HOURS, OR ON WEEKENDS, CALL THE NUMBER SHOWN ABOVE. AN AUTOMATED ATTENDANT PROVIDES AN OPTION CONNECTING THE CALLER TO THE EMERGENCY DUTY DEPUTY.

FRAP 46. ATTORNEYS

(a) *Admission to the Bar.*

(1) *Eligibility.* An attorney is eligible for admission to the bar of a court of appeals if that attorney is of good moral and professional character and is admitted to practice before the Supreme Court of the United States, the highest court of a state, another United States court of appeals, or a United States district court (including the district courts for Guam, the Northern Mariana Islands, and the Virgin Islands).

(2) *Application.* An applicant must file an application for admission, on a form approved by the court that contains the applicant's personal statement showing eligibility for membership. The applicant must subscribe to the following oath or affirmation:

> "I, _____, do solemnly swear [or affirm] that I will conduct myself as an attorney and counselor of this court, uprightly and according to law; and that I will support the Constitution of the United States.

(3) *Admission Procedures.* On written or oral motion of a member of the court's bar, the court will act on the application. An applicant may be admitted by oral motion in open court. But, unless the court orders otherwise, an applicant need not appear before the court to be admitted. Upon admission, an applicant must pay the clerk the fee prescribed by local rule or court order.

(b) *Suspension or Disbarment.*

(1) *Standard.* A member of the court's bar is subject to suspension or disbarment by the court if the member:

(A) has been suspended or disbarred from practice in any other court; or

(B) is guilty of conduct unbecoming a member of the court's bar.

(2) *Procedure.* The member must be given an opportunity to show good cause, within the time prescribed by the court, why the member should not be suspended or disbarred.

(3) *Order.* The court must enter an appropriate order after the member responds and a hearing is held, if requested, or after the time prescribed for a response expires, if no response is made.

(c) ***Discipline.*** A court of appeals may discipline an attorney who practices before it for conduct unbecoming a member of the bar or for failure to comply with any court rule. First, however, the court must afford the attorney reasonable notice, an opportunity to show cause to the contrary, and, if requested, a hearing.

FIFTH CIRCUIT RULE 46

***46.1 Admission and Fees.** Attorneys must have and maintain a valid underlying license to practice law issued by a governmental licensing authority listed in* FED. R. APP. P.*46(a)(1) to be admitted and continue to practice before this court. Admission is governed by* FED. R. APP. P. *46 and this rule. Attorneys admitted to this court must provide the clerk a valid e-mail and mailing address, as well as a working telephone number, and must provide updated information to the clerk when changes occur. Attorneys are admitted for a period of five years and must, after notice from the clerk, timely apply for readmission. To be admitted or readmitted, an attorney must pay the fee fixed by court order. No fee will be required of an attorney who otherwise has all qualifications for admission and is: appointed to represent an appellant in forma pauperis; appearing on behalf of the United States; or newly graduated from law school, licensed to practice in Louisiana, Mississippi, or Texas, and on orders for extended active duty in the Judge Advocate General's Corps.*

***46.2 Suspension or Disbarment.** In addition to* FED. R. APP. P. *46(b), attorneys may be suspended or removed from the roll of attorneys permitted to practice before this court if the appropriate law licensing authority withdraws or suspends the attorney s license to practice law, or the license to practice lapses.*

***46.3 Entry of Appearance.** Attorneys admitted to the bar of this court must enter their appearance in each case in which they participate at the time the case is docketed or upon notice by the clerk. A form for entry of appearance is provided by the clerk. In addition to other pertinent information, the form requires counsel to cite all pending related cases and any cases on the docket of the Supreme Court, or this or any other United States Court of Appeals, which involve a similar issue or issues. Counsel must update such information at the time of briefing. Counsel must also indicate on the form whether the appeal is in a category of cases requiring preference in processing and disposition as set out in* 5TH CIR. R. *47.7.*

I.O.P.- DISCIPLINARY ACTION - FED. R. APP. P. 46(B) AND (C) GOVERN THE PROCEDURES FOLLOWED TO INVOKE DISCIPLINARY ACTION AGAINST ANY MEMBER OF THE BAR OF THIS COURT FOR FAILURE TO COMPLY WITH THE RULES OF THIS COURT, OR FOR CONDUCT UNBECOMING A MEMBER OF THE BAR.

DUTIES OF COURT APPOINTED COUNSEL - THE JUDICIAL COUNCIL OF THE FIFTH CIRCUIT HAS ADOPTED A PLAN UNDER THE CRIMINAL JUSTICE ACT DETAILING THE DUTIES AND

RESPONSIBILITIES OF COURT APPOINTED COUNSEL. A COPY OF THIS PLAN IS AVAILABLE FROM THE CLERK.

AN APPOINTED COUNSEL MAY CLAIM COMPENSATION FOR SERVICES FURNISHED BY A PARTNER OR ASSOCIATE WITHIN THE MAXIMUM COMPENSATION ALLOWED BY THE ACT. HOWEVER, THE COURT EXPECTS COURT-APPOINTED COUNSEL TO TAKE THE LEAD IN PREPARING THE BRIEF AND PRESENTING ORAL ARGUMENT, IF ARGUMENT IS ALLOWED. CLAIMS BY ASSOCIATE COUNSEL FOR IN-COURT SERVICES AND TRAVEL EXPENSES INCURRED IN CONNECTION THEREWITH ARE NOT ALLOWED UNLESS THE PARTNER OR ASSOCIATE IS APPOINTED UNDER THE CRIMINAL JUSTICE ACT ON ADVANCE MOTION AND APPROVAL BY THE COURT.

FRAP 47. LOCAL RULES BY COURTS OF APPEALS

(a) *Local Rules.*

(1) Each court of appeals acting by a majority of its judges in regular active service may, after giving appropriate public notice and opportunity for comment, make and amend rules governing its practice. A generally applicable direction to parties or lawyers regarding practice before a court must be in a local rule rather than an internal operating procedure or standing order. A local rule must be consistent with — but not duplicative of — Acts of Congress and rules adopted under 28 U.S.C. § 2072 and must conform to any uniform numbering system prescribed by the Judicial Conference of the United States. Each circuit clerk must send the Administrative Office of the United States Courts a copy of each local rule and internal operating procedure when it is promulgated or amended.

(2) A local rule imposing a requirement of form must not be enforced in a manner that causes a party to lose rights because of a nonwillful failure to comply with the requirement.

(b) *Procedure When There Is No Controlling Law.* A court of appeals may regulate practice in a particular case in any manner consistent with federal law, these rules, and local rules of the circuit. No sanction or other disadvantage may be imposed for noncompliance with any requirement not in federal law, federal rules, or the local circuit rules unless the alleged violator has been furnished in the particular case with actual notice of the requirement.

FIFTH CIRCUIT RULE 47

OTHER FIFTH CIRCUIT RULES

47.1 Name, Seal and Process.

(a) Name. The name of this court is "United States Court of Appeals for the Fifth Circuit."

(b) Seal. The seal of this court contains the American eagle encircled with the words "United States Court of Appeals" on the upper part of the outer edge; and the words "Fifth Circuit" on the lower part of the outer edge, running from left to right.

(c) Writs and Process. Writs and process of this court are under the seal of the court and signed by the clerk.

47.2 Sessions. *Court sessions are held in each of the states constituting the circuit at least once each year. Sessions may be scheduled at any location having adequate facilities. On motion of a party or on the court s own motion, the court may change the hearing of any appeal to another location or time.*

47.3 Circuit Executive, Library, and Staff Attorneys.

(a) Circuit Executive. The circuit executive s office is maintained at New Orleans, Louisiana. The circuit executive acts as Secretary of the Judicial Council of the Fifth Circuit, provides administrative support to the court, and performs such other duties as the judicial council or the chief judge assigns.

(b) Library. A public library is maintained at New Orleans, Louisiana, which is open during hours fixed by the court. Books and materials may not be removed from the library without permission of the librarian. Other libraries may be maintained at such places in the circuit as the court designates.

(c) Staff Attorneys. A central staff of attorneys is maintained at New Orleans, Louisiana, to perform such research and record analysis as the court directs.

47.4 Bankruptcy Appeals.

47.4.1 The FED. R. APP. P. *and 5*TH CIR. R. *apply to all appeals from United States Bankruptcy Courts to this court.*

47.4.2 Appeals docketed in the district court or with the clerk of any authorized appellate panels, may not be transferred to this court unless the district judge or appellate panel approves the transfer in writing.

47.5 Publication of Opinions.

47.5.1 Criteria for Publication. The publication of opinions that merely decide particular cases on the basis of well-settled principles of law imposes needless expense on the public and burdens on the legal profession. However, opinions that may in any way interest persons other than the parties to a case should be published. Therefore, an opinion is published if it:

(a) Establishes a new rule of law, alters, or modifies an existing rule of law, or calls attention to an existing rule of law that appears to have been generally overlooked;

(b) Applies an established rule of law to facts significantly different from those in previous published opinions applying the rule;

(c) Explains, criticizes, or reviews the history of existing decisional or enacted law;

(d) Creates or resolves a conflict of authority either within the circuit or between this circuit and another;

(e) Concerns or discusses a factual or legal issue of significant public interest; or

(f) Is rendered in a case that has been reviewed previously and its merits addressed by an opinion of the United States Supreme Court.

An opinion may also be published if it:

> *Is accompanied by a concurring or dissenting opinion; or reverses the decision below or affirms it upon different grounds.*

47.5.2   Publication Decision. An opinion will be published unless each member of the panel deciding the case determines that its publication is neither required nor justified under the criteria for publication. If any judge of the court or any party so requests the panel will reconsider its decision not to publish an opinion. The opinion will be published if, upon reconsideration, each member of the panel determines that it meets one or more of the criteria for publication or should be published for any other good reason, and the panel issues an order to publish the opinion.

47.5.3   Unpublished Opinions Issued Before January 1, 1996*. Unpublished opinions issued before January 1, 1996*, are precedent. Although every opinion believed to have precedential value is published, an unpublished opinion may be cited pursuant to FED. R. APP. P. 32.1(a). The party citing to an unpublished judicial disposition must provide a citation to the disposition in a publicly accessible electronic database. If the disposition is not available in an electronic database, a copy of any unpublished opinion cited in any document being submitted to the court, must be attached to each copy of the document, as required by FED. R. APP. P. 32.1(b).

47.5.4   Unpublished Opinions Issued on or After January 1, 1996*. Unpublished opinions issued on or after January 1, 1996*, are not precedent, except under the doctrine of res judicata, collateral estoppel or law of the case (or similarly to show double jeopardy, notice, sanctionable conduct, entitlement to attorney's fees, or the like). An unpublished opinion may be cited pursuant to FED. R. APP. P. 32.1(a). The party citing to an unpublished judicial disposition should provide a citation to the disposition in a publicly accessible electronic database. If the disposition is not available in an electronic database, a copy of any unpublished opinion cited in any document being submitted to the court must be attached to

---

*Effective date of amended Rule.

each copy of the document, as required by FED. R. APP. P. *32.1(b). The first page of each unpublished opinion bears the following legend:*

> *Pursuant to* 5TH CIRCUIT RULE *47.5, the court has determined that this opinion should not be published and is not precedent except under the limited circumstances set forth in* 5TH CIRCUIT RULE *47.5.4.*

47.5.5 Definition of Published. An opinion is considered as published for purposes of this rule when the panel deciding the case determines, in accordance with 5TH CIR. R. *47.5.2, that the opinion will be published and the opinion is issued.*

47.6 Affirmance Without Opinion. *The judgment or order may be affirmed or enforced without opinion when the court determines that an opinion would have no precedential value and that any one or more of the following circumstances exists and is dispositive of a matter submitted for decision: (1) that a judgment of the district court is based on findings of fact that are not clearly erroneous; (2) that the evidence in support of a jury verdict is not insufficient; (3) that the order of an administrative agency is supported by substantial evidence on the record as a whole; (4) in the case of a summary judgment, that no genuine issue of material fact has been properly raised by the appellant; and (5) no reversible error of law appears. In such case, the court may, in its discretion, enter either of the following orders: AFFIRMED. See* 5TH CIR. R. *47.6. or ENFORCED. See* 5TH CIR. R. *47.6.*

47.7 Calendaring Priorities. *The following categories of cases are given preference in processing and disposition: (1) appeals in criminal cases, (2) habeas corpus petitions and motions attacking a federal sentence, (3) proceedings involving recalcitrant witnesses before federal courts or grand juries under 28 U.S.C. § 1826, (4) actions for temporary or preliminary injunctive relief, and (5) any other action if good cause therefor is shown. (*FED. R. APP. P. *45(b) and 28 U.S.C. § 1657).*

47.8 Attorney's Fees.

47.8.1 Supporting Requirements. Petitions or motions for the award of attorney's fees should always be supported by contemporaneous time records recording all work for which a fee is claimed and reflecting the hours or fractional hours of work done and the specific professional level of services performed by each lawyer seeking compensation. In the absence of such records, time expended will not be considered in setting the fee beyond the minimum amount necessary in the court's judgment for any lawyer to produce the work seen in court. Exceptions may be made only to avoid an unconscionable result.

The clerk will make reasonable efforts to advise counsel about this rule, but whether or not counsel has been advised, ignorance of this rule is not, standing alone, grounds for an exception. If the reasonableness of the hours claimed on the basis of time records becomes an issue, the applicant must make time records available for inspection by opposing counsel and, if a dispute is not resolved between them, by the court.

47.8.2 Attorney s Fees and Expenses Under the Equal Access to Justice Act. This rule implements the provisions of the Equal Access to Justice Act, Public Law No. 96-481, 94 Stat. 2325 (1980).

- *(a) Applications to the Court of Appeals. An application for an award of fees and expenses pursuant to 28 U.S.C. § 2412(d)(1)(B) must identify the applicant and the proceeding for which an award is sought. The application must show the nature and extent of services provided in this court and that the applicant has prevailed, and must identify the position of the United States or an agency thereof that the applicant alleges was not substantially justified.*

- *(b) Petitions by Permission. A petition for leave to appeal pursuant to 5 U.S.C. § 504(c)(2) must be filed with the clerk of the court of appeals within 30 days after the entry of the agency's order, with proof of service on all other parties to the agency's proceedings.*

- *(c) The petition must contain a copy of the order to be reviewed and any findings of fact, conclusions of law, and opinion relating thereto, a statement of the facts necessary to an understanding of the petition, and a memorandum showing why the petition for permission to appeal should be granted. An answer may be filed within 30 days after service of the petition, unless otherwise directed by the court. The application and any answer will be submitted without further briefing and oral argument unless otherwise ordered.*

- *(d) An original and 3 copies must be filed with the court.*

- *(e) Within 10 days after the entry of an order granting permission to appeal, the applicant must pay the clerk of this court the docket fee prescribed by the Judicial Conference of the United States. Upon receipt of the payment, the clerk will enter the appeal upon the docket. The record shall be transmitted and filed in accordance with FED. R. APP. P. 17. A notice of appeal need not be filed.*

- *(f) Appeals/Petitions to Review. Appeals and petitions to review matters otherwise contemplated by the Equal Access to Justice Act may be filed pursuant to the applicable statutes and rules of the court.*

47.9 Rules for the Conduct of Proceedings Under the Judicial Conduct and Disability Act, 28 U.S.C. §§ 351 et seq.

See separately published Judicial Council of the Fifth Circuit Rules Governing Complaints of Judicial Misconduct or Disability effective April 15, 1993 as amended through May 4, 2008.

47.10 Rule Governing Appeals Raising Sentencing Guidelines Issues - 18 U.S.C. § 3742.

47.10.1   *Scope of Rules.* These rules govern procedures in appeals raising sentencing issues pursuant to 18 U.S.C. § 3742(a) or (b). These cases will proceed in the same manner and under the general rules of court governing other appeals and will not be given special expedited treatment over other criminal cases, except as hereinafter specified.

47.10.2   *Motion to Expedite.* If the defendant is incarcerated for a period of 1 year or less pursuant to the sentence appealed, a party may file a motion to expedite the appeal upon a showing of irreparable harm. The motion must set out: (a) when the trial transcript can be prepared and made available; and, (b) how soon thereafter appellant can file a brief. The court disfavors bifurcation of issues concerning sentencing from those issues involving the conviction.

47.10.3   *The Appellate Record.*

(a) *Oral Reasons for Imposition of Sentence.* The oral statement of reasons of the district court for imposition of a sentence as required by 18 U.S.C. § 3553(c), as amended, must be reduced to writing, filed, and incorporated in the record on appeal.

(b) *Transcript of Sentencing Proceedings.* In addition to the requirements of FED. R. APP. P. 10(b) and 5TH CIR. R. 10.1 for ordering the transcript of trial proceedings, appellant is required to order a transcript of the entire sentencing proceeding (excluding the oral statement of reasons for sentencing of the district court) if a sentencing issue under 18 U.S.C. § 3742 will be raised on appeal.

(c) *Presentence Report.* If a notice of appeal is filed as authorized by 18 U.S.C. § 3742(a) and (b) for review of a sentence, the clerk will transmit to this court the presentence report. The report is transmitted separately from other parts of the record on appeal and is labeled as a sealed record if sealed by the district court.

(d) Presentence reports filed in this court as part of a record on appeal are treated as matters of public record except where the report, or a portion thereof was sealed by order of the district court.

(e) *Counsel wishing access to, or a copy of, sealed presentence reports, or portions of such reports, may request them from the clerk's office by such means as the clerk permits. Counsel must return the copy of the presentence report, without duplicating it. Counsel should avoid disclosure of confidential matters in their public filings.*

FRAP 48. MASTERS

(a) *Appointment; Powers.* A court of appeals may appoint a special master to hold hearings, if necessary, and to recommend factual findings and disposition in matters ancillary to proceedings in the court. Unless the order referring a matter to a master specifies or limits the master's powers, those powers include, but are not limited to, the following:

(1) regulating all aspects of a hearing;

(2) taking all appropriate action for the efficient performance of the master's duties under the order;

(3) requiring the production of evidence on all matters embraced in the reference; and

(4) administering oaths and examining witnesses and parties.

(b) *Compensation.* If the master is not a judge or court employee, the court must determine the master s compensation and whether the cost is to be charged to any party.

OTHER INTERNAL OPERATING PROCEDURES

JUDICIAL COUNCIL - The judicial council established by 28 U.S.C. § 332 is composed of 19 judges - the chief circuit judge, nine circuit judges, and nine district judges. The chief circuit judge and the active circuit judge next in seniority serve permanent terms. All other council members serve for staggered three-year terms. The council meets on call of the chief circuit judge pursuant to statute.

JUDICIAL CONFERENCE - Pursuant to 28 U.S.C. § 333, the chief circuit judge may summon biennially or annually the federal judges of the circuit to a conference, at a designated time and place, for the purpose of considering the state of business of the courts and advising means of improving the administration of justice within the circuit. A copy of the court s rule for representation and active participation of the members of the bar of the circuit is available from the clerk or circuit executive.

RECUSAL OR DISQUALIFICATION OF JUDGES

(A) GROUNDS - Judges may recuse themselves under any circumstances considered sufficient to require such action. Judges must disqualify themselves under circumstances set forth in 28 U.S.C. § 455, or in accordance with Canon 3C, Code of Conduct for United States Judges as adopted by the Judicial Conference of the United States.

(B) PROCEDURE

   (1) ADMINISTRATIVE MOTIONS - If an initiating judge recuses himself or herself from considering, or is disqualified to consider an administrative motion, he or she will notify the clerk, who will advise the recused judge of the next initiating judge and request that the file be sent to that judge.

   (2) SUMMARY CALENDAR CASES - The above procedure is followed, except that the substitute or backup judge is called because it is court practice that cases are not ordinarily disposed of on the merits by only 2 judges.

   (3) HEARING CALENDAR CASES - Prior to the formal publication of the court calendar, each judge on the panel is furnished with a copy of the 5th Cir. R. 28.2.1 certificate of interested persons for the judge's study to determine whether recusal or disqualification is appropriate.

(C) If a judge recuses, or is disqualified, he or she immediately notifies the other members of the panel, and arrangements are made for a substitute judge.

SPECIAL PANELS AND CASES REQUIRING SPECIAL HANDLING

Corporate Reorganization - Chapter 11

The first appeal is handled in the usual manner. Counsel must state in their briefs whether the proceeding is likely to be complex and protracted so that the panel can determine whether it should enter an order directing that it will be the permanent panel for subsequent appeals in the same matter. If there are likely to be successive appeals, a single panel may thus become fully familiar with the case thus making the handling of future appeals more expeditious and economical for litigants, counsel and the court. (For the rule regarding direct appeals in bankruptcy matters see 5th Cir. R. 47.4).

Criminal Justice Act Plan - The court has adopted a plan and guidelines under the Criminal Justice Act. Copies are available from the clerk.

Certified Records for Supreme Court of the United States - The clerk's office does not prepare a certified record unless the Clerk of the United States Supreme Court so directs. (See generally Sup. Ct. R. 12.7, 16.2, and 19.4).

Building Security

(A) Reasons for Building Security - These rules are to minimize interference with and disruptions of the court's business, to preserve decorum in conducting the court's business and to provide effective security in the John Minor Wisdom United States Court of Appeals Building and garage located at 600 Camp Street, and court occupied space at 600 S. Maestri Place, New Orleans, Louisiana. These entire premises are called The Buildings.

(B) Security Personnel - The term Security Personnel means the U.S. Marshal or Deputy Marshal, Court Security Officer, or a member of the Federal Protective Service Police.

(C) Carrying of Parcels, Bags, and Other Objects - Security Personnel shall inspect all objects carried by persons entering The Buildings. No one shall enter or remain in The Buildings without submitting to an inspection.

(D) SEARCH OF PERSONS - SECURITY PERSONNEL MAY SEARCH ANY PERSON ENTERING THE BUILDINGS OR ANY SPACE IN IT. ANYONE WHO REFUSES A SEARCH MUST BE DENIED ENTRY.

(E) UNSEEMLY CONDUCT - NO PERSON SHALL:

  (1) LOITER, SLEEP OR CONDUCT ONESELF IN AN UNSEEMLY OR DISORDERLY MANNER IN THE BUILDINGS;

  (2) INTERFERE WITH OR DISTURB THE CONDUCT OF THE COURT S BUSINESS IN ANY MANNER;

  (3) EAT OR DRINK IN THE HALLS OF THE BUILDINGS OR IN ANY COURTROOMS EXCEPT AT COURT APPROVED SOCIAL FUNCTIONS;

  (4) BLOCK ANY ENTRANCE TO OR EXIT FROM THE BUILDING OR INTERFERE IN ANY PERSON'S ENTRY INTO OR EXIT FROM THE BUILDING.

(F) ENTERING AND LEAVING - ALL PERSONS MUST ENTER AND LEAVE COURTROOMS ONLY THROUGH SUCH DOORWAYS AND AT SUCH TIMES AS ARE DESIGNATED BY THE SECURITY PERSONNEL.

(G) SPECTATORS - THE ENTRANCE AND DEPARTURE OF SPECTATORS TO OR FROM COURTROOMS IS SUBJECT TO THE PRESIDING JUDGE S DIRECTIONS. THE U. S. MARSHAL MAY DESIGNATE SPECTATOR SEATING IN ANY COURTROOM. SPECTATORS EXCLUDED BECAUSE OF LACK OF SEATING AND SPECTATORS LEAVING THE COURTROOM WHILE COURT IS IN SESSION OR ANY RECESS SHALL NOT LOITER OR REMAIN IN THE AREA ADJACENT TO THE COURTROOM.

(H) CAMERAS AND ELECTRONIC EQUIPMENT - NO PERSON SHALL INTRODUCE OR ATTEMPT TO INTRODUCE ANY TYPE OF CAMERA, RECORDING EQUIPMENT, OR OTHER TYPE OF ELECTRICAL OR ELECTRONIC DEVICE INTO THE BUILDINGS WITHOUT THE COURT'S PERMISSION.

(I) WEAPONS - EXCEPT FOR SECURITY PERSONNEL, NO PERSON SHALL BE ADMITTED TO OR ALLOWED TO REMAIN IN THE BUILDINGS WITH ANY OBJECT THAT MIGHT BE EMPLOYED AS A WEAPON UNLESS AUTHORIZED IN WRITING BY THE COURT TO DO SO.

(J) ENFORCEMENT - SECURITY PERSONNEL SHALL ENFORCE THESE SECURITY PROVISIONS AND ANY OTHER PROVISIONS THE COURT MIGHT IMPLEMENT. ATTORNEYS AND PARTIES WHO VIOLATE THESE PROVISIONS ARE SUBJECT TO, INTER ALIA, CONTEMPT PROCEEDINGS AND SANCTIONS.

FED. R. APP. P. WITH 5TH CIR. R. & IOPs

APPENDIX OF FORMS

FORM 1. NOTICE OF APPEAL TO A COURT OF APPEALS FROM A JUDGMENT OR ORDER OF A DISTRICT COURT

United States District Court for the
_____District of _____

File Number _____

A.B., Plaintiff }
}
v. }
} Notice of Appeal
}
C.D., Defendant }

Notice is hereby given that ____(here name all parties taking the appeal)___, (plaintiffs) (defendants) in the above named case,* hereby appeal to the United States Court of Appeals for the _____Circuit (from the final judgment) (from an order (describing it)) entered in this action on the ___ day of _____, 20__.

(s)_____

Attorney for_____

Address:_____

* See Rule 3(c) for permissible ways of identifying appellants.

FED. R. APP. P. WITH 5TH CIR. R. & IOPs

FORM 2. NOTICE OF APPEAL TO A COURT OF APPEALS FROM A DECISION OF THE UNITED STATES TAX COURT

UNITED STATES TAX COURT
Washington, D.C.

A.B., Petitioner }
}
v. } Docket No._____
}
Commissioner of Internal }
Revenue, Respondent }

Notice of Appeal

Notice is hereby given that _(here name all parties taking the appeal) *_ hereby appeal to the United States Court of Appeals for the _____ Circuit from (that part of) the decision of this court entered in the above captioned proceeding on the ___day of _____, 20__ (relating to _____).

(s)_____

Counsel for_____

Address:_____

* See Rule 3(c) for permissible ways of identifying appellants.

FED. R. APP. P. WITH 5TH CIR. R. & IOPs

FORM 3. PETITION FOR REVIEW OF ORDER OF AN AGENCY, BOARD, COMMISSION OR OFFICER

United States Court of Appeals
for the _____ Circuit

A.B., Petitioner　}
　　　　　　　　　}
　　v.　　　　　　} Petition for Review
XYZ Commission,　}
Respondent　　　　}

　　__(here name all parties bringing the petition)*__ hereby petition the court for review of the Order of the XYZ Commission (describe the order) entered on _____, 20__.

(s)_____
Attorney for Petitioners

Address:_____

* See Rule 15.

FED. R. APP. P. WITH 5TH CIR. R. & IOPs

FORM 4 AFFIDAVIT ACCOMPANYING MOTION FOR PERMISSION TO APPEAL IN FORMA PAUPERIS

United States District Court for the   District of

A.B., Plaintiff

v.   Case No._____

C.D., Defendant

My issues on appeal are:

1. For both you and your spouse estimate the average amount of money received from each of the following sources during the past 12 months. Adjust any amount that was received weekly, biweekly, quarterly, semiannually, or annually to show the monthly rate. Use gross amounts, that is, amounts before any deductions for taxes or otherwise.

Income source	Average monthly amount during the past 12 months You	Amount expected next month You
Employment	$_____	$_____
Self-employment	$_____	$_____
Income from real property (such as rental income)	$_____	$_____
Interest and dividends	$_____	$_____
Gifts	$_____	$_____
Alimony	$_____	$_____
Child support	$_____	$_____
Retirement (such as social security, pensions, annuities, insurance)	$_____	$_____
Disability (such as social security, insurance payments)	$_____	$_____
Unemployment payments	$_____	$_____
Public assistance (such as welfare)	$_____	$_____
Other (specify):	$_____	$_____
Total monthly income:	$_____	$_____

MISC-14

2. List your employment history, most recent employer first. (Gross monthly pay is before taxes or other deductions.)

Employer	Address	Dates of Employment	Gross monthly pay
_____	_____	_____	_____
_____	_____	_____	_____
_____	_____	_____	_____

3. List your spouse's employment history, most recent employer first. (Gross monthly pay is before taxes or other deductions.)

Employer	Address	Dates of Employment	Gross monthly pay
_____	_____	_____	_____
_____	_____	_____	_____
_____	_____	_____	_____

4. How much cash do you and your spouse have? $_____

Below, state any money you or your spouse have in bank accounts or in any other financial institution.

Financial institution	Type of account	Amount you have	Amount your spouse has
_____	_____	$_____	$_____
_____	_____	$_____	$_____
_____	_____	$_____	$_____

If you are a prisoner, you must attach a statement certified by the appropriate institutional officer showing all receipts, expenditures, and balances during the last six months in your institutional accounts. If you have multiple accounts, perhaps because you have been in multiple institutions, attach one certified statement of each account.

5. List the assets, and their values, which you own or your spouse owns. Do not list clothing and ordinary household furnishings.

Home	(Value)	Other real estate (Value)	Motor vehicle #1 (Value)
_____		_____	Make & year:_____
_____		_____	Model:_____
_____		_____	Registration #_____

MISC-14

FED. R. APP. P. WITH 5TH CIR. R. & IOPs

Motor vehicle #2 (Value)   Other assets (Value)   Other assets (Value)

Make & year:_____   _____   _____

Model:_____   _____   _____

Registration #:_____   _____   _____

6. State every person, business, or organization owing you or your spouse money, and the amount owed.

Person owing you or your spouse money	Amount owed to you	Amount owed to your spouse
_____	_____	_____
_____	_____	_____
_____	_____	_____

7. State the persons who rely on you or your spouse for support.

Name (or, if under 18, initials only)	Relationship	Age
_____	_____	_____
_____	_____	_____
_____	_____	_____

8. Estimate the average monthly expenses of you and your family. Show separately the amounts paid by your spouse. Adjust any payments that are made weekly, biweekly, quarterly, semiannually, or annually to show the monthly rate.

	You	Your Spouse

Rent or home-mortgage payment (include lot rented for mobile home)
    Are real-estate taxes included? 9 Yes 9 No
    Is property insurance included? 9 Yes 9 No
	$_____	$_____

Utilities (electricity, heating fuel, water, sewer, and Telephone)	$_____	$_____
Home maintenance (repairs and upkeep)	$_____	$_____
Food	$_____	$_____
Clothing	$_____	$_____
Laundry and dry-cleaning	$_____	$_____
Medical and dental expenses	$_____	$_____
Transportation (not including motor vehicle payments)	$_____	$_____
Recreation, entertainment, newspapers, magazines, etc.	$_____	$_____
Insurance (not deducted from wages or included in Mortgage payments)	$_____	$_____

MISC-14

Homeowner's or renter's	$_____	$_____
Life	$_____	$_____
Health	$_____	$_____
Motor Vehicle	$_____	$_____
Other: _____	$_____	$_____

Taxes (not deducted from wages or included in Mortgage payments) (specify): _____ $_____ $_____

Installment payments $_____ $_____

   Motor Vehicle $_____ $_____

      Credit card (name): _____ $_____ $_____

      Department store (name): _____ $_____ $_____

      Other: _____ $_____ $_____

Alimony, maintenance, and support paid to others $_____ $_____

Regular expenses for operation of business, profession, or farm (attach detailed statement) $_____ $_____

Other (specify): _____ $_____ $_____

Total monthly expenses: $_____ $_____

9. Do you expect any major changes to your monthly income or expenses or in your assets or liabilities during the next 12 months?

❏ Yes ❏ No   If yes, describe on an attached sheet.

10. Have you paid — or will you be paying — an attorney any money for services in connection with this case, including the completion of this form? ❏ Yes ❏ No

If yes, how much? $_____

If yes, state the attorney's name, address, and telephone number:

_____

_____

_____

11. Have you paid — or will you be paying — anyone other than an attorney (such as a paralegal or a typist) any money for services in connection with this case, including the completion of this form?

❏ Yes ❏ No

If yes, how much? $_____

If yes, state the person's name, address, and telephone number:

_____

_____

MISC-14

12. Provide any other information that will help explain why you cannot pay the docket fees for your appeal.

13. State the [city and state] of your legal residence.

_____

_____

Your daytime phone number: (_____) _____

Your age: _____ Your years of schooling: _____

[Last four digits of] your social-security number: _____

FORM 5. NOTICE OF APPEAL TO A COURT OF APPEALS FROM A JUDGMENT OR ORDER OF A DISTRICT COURT OR A BANKRUPTCY APPELLATE PANEL

United States District Court for the
_____District of _____

In re

_____,

Debtor

_____,

Plaintiff   File No._____

v.

_____,

Defendant

Notice of Appeal to
United States Court of Appeals
for the _____Circuit

_____, the plaintiff [or defendant or other party] appeals to the United States Court of Appeals for the _____ Circuit from the final judgment [or order or decree] of the district court for the district of _____ [or bankruptcy appellate panel of the _____ circuit], entered in this case on _____, 20__ [here describe the judgment, order, or decree] _____.

The parties to the judgment [or order or decree] appealed from and the names and addresses of their respective attorneys are as follows:

Dated _____

Signed _____
Attorney for Appellant

Address: _____

_____

FORM 6. CERTIFICATE OF COMPLIANCE WITH RULE 32(a)

Certificate of Compliance with Type-Volume Limitation,
Typeface Requirements, and Type Style Requirements

1. This brief complies with the type-volume limitation of FED. R. APP. P. 32(a)(7)(B) because:

  ☐ this brief contains [*state the number of*] words, excluding the parts of the brief exempted by FED. R. APP. P. 32(a)(7)(B)(iii), *or*

  ☐ this brief uses a monospaced typeface and contains [*state the number of*] lines of text, excluding the parts of the brief exempted by FED. R. APP. P. 32(a)(7)(B)(iii).

2. This brief complies with the typeface requirements of FED. R. APP. P. 32(a)(5) and the type style requirements of FED. R. APP. P. 32(a)(6) because:

  ☐ this brief has been prepared in a proportionally spaced typeface using [*state name and version of word processing program*] in [*state font size and name of type style*], *or*

  ☐ this brief has been prepared in a monospaced typeface using [*state name and version of word processing program*] with [*state number of characters per inch and name of type style*].

(s)_____

Attorney for_____

Dated:_____

Made in the USA
Coppell, TX
25 January 2022